W9-AMP-762

FIRESIDE
PARKSIDE

FIRESIDE PARKSIDE BOOKS

Blues Ain't Nothing But a Good Soul Feeling Bad

A Pilgrimage to Inner Peace

Sheldon Kopp

with Bonnie B. Hesse

A FIRESIDE/PARKSIDE RECOVERY BOOK
Published by Simon & Schuster

New York   London   Toronto   Tokyo
Sydney   Singapore

FIRESIDE/PARKSIDE
Rockefeller Center
1230 Avenue of the Americas
New York, New York 10020

3   5   7   9   10   8   6   4   2

Library of Congress Cataloging-in-Publication Data

Kopp, Sheldon B., 1929–
Blues ain't nothing but a good soul feeling bad : a pilgrimage to inner peace /
Sheldon Kopp with Bonnie B. Hesse.
p.   cm.
Includes index.
1. Meditations.   I. Hesse, Bonnie B.   II. Title.
BL624.2.K66   1991
291.4′3—dc20   91-29302
                                                        CIP

ISBN: 0-671-76838-7

Designed by Irving Perkins Associates
Manufactured in the United States of America

Parkside Medical Services Corporation is a full-service
provider of treatment for alcoholism, other drug addiction,
eating disorders, and psychiatric illness.

Parkside Medical Services Corporation
205 West Touhy Avenue
Park Ridge, IL 60058
1-800-PARKSIDE

*No matter how confident we feel about the out-
come of our actions or how well we prepare for
an event, the moment belongs to God. We need
to accept the holy insecurity of living without
certainty and yet with faith and humor.*
—SHELDON KOPP

EDITOR'S NOTE

SINCE the publication of *If You Meet the Buddha on the Road, Kill Him!*, Sheldon Kopp has led us, insisting that we not be followers, on a search for real lives of our own. His precise vision of who we are not—and what no one can do—deleted the pretense and illusion separating us from reality. So, we found ourselves standing beside him, starkly disarmed, as unique but ordinary human beings, faced with the primal choice to do something honest and real or to do something worth nothing at all, or worse. *If You Meet the Buddha . . .* is still studied in major universities, still read and reread by those who continue to be transformed by it.

Admitting his vulnerability, exposing his absurdity, and confessing his profanity, Kopp claimed for himself what goodness he could out of who he was. Incidentally he provided a critical catalyst for the rest of us: We came to believe that, as flawed as we may be, it is humanly possible to face our own darkness and learn to accept all that we are. That was, and still is, the requisite first step to any possible personal peace.

Though his many subsequent books have dealt with various issues, he returns here to the essence of "the Buddha book"—that we have to do the most important things for ourselves, no excuses accepted.

Using the one-day-at-a-time format, Kopp poses thoughts and questions, but the only right answers are of our own making. His writings are new, extracted largely from his journals, but some of his most memorable lines have been repeated simply because he felt like it, and so did we.

To those of you who are new to Sheldon Kopp's relentlessly confrontive, startlingly honest, intelligent, loving, and committed pursuit of partial dignity and a measure of peace, serendipity is the watchword. You may discover, as so many others have declared, "His books changed my life."

—Bonnie Hesse

INTRODUCTION

INNER PEACE is as elusive as it is desirable. Much of the time, we feel restless, discontent, or needlessly upset. Paradoxically, to find what peace we can, we must endure feeling unsettled while we search for answers to what the Hasidic teachers call the "holy insecurities," challenging questions that keep us in touch with our responsibility for who we are and how we live.

Although we may find ourselves in different situations throughout our lives, again and again these same themes recur and repeatedly challenge us to reconsider our basic beliefs and ways of being. The brief thoughts offered on the following pages are reflections on topics that concern us all—suffering, fear, weakness, love, trust, and unmanageable lives.

Four central, universal questions or holy insecurities are the central themes for the four parts of this book:

> *Part 1—How do I find a self of my own?*
> *Part 2—Where am I in my life?*
> *Part 3—Who am I in my world?*
> *Part 4—Where do I go from here?*

If we have the humility to accept uncertainty and the willingness to live with the creative tension between certainty and doubt, we can open our minds to the words of our hearts and hear the voice of our higher power. Only then will we be able to deepen our souls' understanding so that we can take the needed steps to experience a growing sense of inner peace—a still-point at the center of our selves that protects us from avoidable suffering.

—Sheldon Kopp

1

HOW DO I FIND
A SELF OF MY OWN?

*Strengthened by desire and hope, burdened by
anxiety and fear, beset by temptations and
guarded by spiritual powers, [the seeker] pur-
sues his way along the Path of Life, seeking ever
"a better country."*

—SAMUEL CLAGGET CHEW

*The solitary path to the depth of our souls first
leads us to the edge of our aloneness, and only
then back to a place among others—a place
that is truly our own*

—SHELDON KOPP

January 1

JUST BEFORE Gertrude Stein died, she asked, "What is the answer?" When none of the friends gathered at her bedside replied, she laughed, and said, "In that case, what is the question?" Then she died.

These conundrums about the meaning of life captivate us at times of crises, but they reside in the shadows of our lives even when we are not attending to them. These questions often occur in the following form: "How do I find a self of my own?"; "Where am I in my life?"; "Where am I in my world?"; and "Where do I go from here?" The answers come in many forms, depending on who in particular is asking, and in which situation, and to what end.

The questions are the same. It is only the answers that change.

IN *A Brief History of Time*, renowned physicist Stephen Hawking poses problems that expand our minds. Reporting that St. Augustine was once asked, "What did God do before he created the universe?" Hawking wryly suggests the answer might have been, "He was preparing Hell for people who asked such questions."

Hawking explains that "ever since the dawn of civilization, people . . . have craved an understanding of the underlying order in the world. Today we still yearn to know why we are here and where we came from." He goes on to say that the goal of science is to provide a single theory to describe the whole universe, but that is an indescribably difficult task, and the partial theories we have are good enough for all practical purposes.

Obviously, we have no choice but to use what we know for sure as a basis for accepting and living with what we may never know. Still, we may well consider the value of the uncertainties. What would we do if we knew all the answers?

The questions that keep us searching may be more captivating than the answers we seek.

January 3

WHAT SORT of a world is this? Too often it seems a lunatic life filled with suffering, devoid of meaning. Yet, it is all the world there is. We can only choose to live life as it is. Complaining about it is part of living, but we can't hope that our complaining will improve anything.

Here then is the message each of us must send to ourselves: I can only become who I am. And I can only live this particular life that I have been given. The only meaning for me is to go on, feeling it all, discovering as much of it as I can take in, seeking not improvement or even change but the courage to see it all, every last detail. When I reach out to others to hear their cry, I know that it is not to cure them but to heal myself.

If we are willing to endure the holy insecurities, we can find the higher power within us.

"WHY AM I afraid to tell you who I am?" asks John Powell in his important book by that name. He quotes one young person's answer: "I am afraid to tell you who I am, because if I tell you who I am, you might not like who I am, and that is all I have." As frightening as it is to reveal ourselves to others, we must risk it or live alone.

Being committed to revealing our true selves is a never-ending struggle, for each and every one of us is, at times, awful and wonderful, good and bad, peculiar and ordinary. However, the more we can accept and honor our own contrasts, our darkness and our light, the more we will come to believe in the possibility that others can love us as well. As Walt Whitman wrote in "Song of Myself":

> *I am large, I contain multitudes.*
> *Do I contradict myself?*
> *Very well then, I contradict myself.*

Learning to love yourself opens the way for others to do the same.

January 5

THERE ARE some old lessons that must be learned again and again.

Acquiring wisdom involves the risk of being wrong or foolish

Being loving and tender requires a willingness to bear unhappiness

Courage is the confidence to face danger, even though afraid

Gaining freedom and power requires only a willingness to recognize their existence and face their consequences

We can find ourselves only when we are willing to risk losing ourselves to another, to the moment, to a quest, and love is the bridge

There are no wizards, no buddhas, no gods among us; the only one on earth who knows your answers is you.

The secret is there is no secret.

"TURNING" STANDS at the very heart of the Jewish conception of a person's way in the world. Each one must face up not only on the Day of Atonement but at each moment. Each present moment is a moment of redemption. As Rabbi Bunam said, "Our greatest crime is not that we sin, but that we can turn every moment and do not."

But then, how are we to face up to daily frustrations and frequent disappointments, betrayal by people we trust and loss of people we love? At times we need help, a hand extended to us. Even so, the searching of the heart must involve a genuine willingness to face up to our losses, accept that what we have been through we cannot change, and commit to things as they must be. In this way, we can renew ourselves from within.

When is the proper time for this turning? If not now, when?

January 7

EVERYONE EXPERIENCES times when life seems so out of control there is nothing we can do to make things right. When we go through these unsettling episodes, we feel like helpless victims of arbitrary fate.

The days of being upset over trivial troubles seem bad enough, but they pale by comparison when there is a serious crisis that threatens to disrupt our lives completely. During these terrible occasions, later remembered as "the worst times of our lives," much that gives meaning to our lives appears to be in jeopardy.

In circumstances like these over which you have no control, there is little more you can do except stand by patiently and hope for the best. Faced with the reality that no one is ever totally safe from harm, you sometimes have to settle for assuming an attitude that makes your powerlessness more bearable.

Coping with helplessness is one kind of power.

AMONG THE Ojibwa, an American Indian tribe, when it came time, a father led his son into the woods to leave him to fast, to be alone, and to ponder the meaning of life. Since this was to be a time of self-discovery, the boy was not told what he might expect to encounter. No socially approved image was offered to him. Rather, he was given the understanding that he would have a vision, his own vision of who he was to be and what he was to do with his life.

The boy going through this initiation rite was told that whatever this vision was, whatever he learned about himself and the world, should be trusted and accepted. When he returned, his vision would be honored by the tribe, simply because it was his and because he had discovered it for himself and claimed it as his own.

We need time alone to discover who we really are.

January 9

WORK ON the self requires the clear development of a set of internal personal standards for determining what is important to you. Relying on the standards and expectations of others leaves us vulnerable to follow the trends of the moment or the conventions of the crowd.

What's to be done if we don't meet others' expectations or our own? Ram Dass suggests "that it all has to do with how I define who I am and if I define myself as somebody that's hurtable, then everybody can potentially hurt me. On the other hand, if I'm somebody who is just here, watching the dance of life . . . there's very little anybody can do to me. It's the question of how deep into your center you are about yourself [where] you can watch your own personality drama with a little less attachment to it."

Part of the work on ourselves is simply taking the role of a nonjudgmental, loving witness to our lives.

THE PHRASE "turning our lives over to a higher power" creates a major stumbling block for some people when they are seeking spiritual solace. These words commonly conjure up notions of giving up control ourselves or being told what to do by someone else.

In life there are few answers, many mysteries, and more questions. But some conclusions can safely be drawn about what "turning our lives over" does *not* mean. It does not involve giving up control over your life. You can't give up what you never had, but you can take charge of yourself by acknowledging how little control you have over everything else.

Turning your life over doesn't mean giving up responsibility for who you are and how you act. If anything, it means taking more responsibility, not less; it means gaining inner power, not losing it.

By consciously connecting with your higher power, you give in to your own, true inner voice and give up all that was false and not you. The paradox is that in turning over your life, you are getting your own life back.

Ultimately, faith implies surrender to yourself.

January 11

YOU MAY be able to fool even those people who mean the most to you. Knowing only those parts of you that you *choose* to reveal to them, they *seem* to care. But what would happen if they should discover what you are like when nothing is hidden in the shadows? If they really knew you, would they still care?

Letting your self be known means taking a chance, but hiding out can be just as risky. To the extent that you succeed in deceiving others, you are stuck with secret feelings that some others might be able to accept, and with the hidden qualities that some might even value. Worse yet, when you succeed in deceiving others, you are isolated and alone.

If no one knows you, who can love you?

SOME OF us were abused or neglected when we were children. Our parents' attitudes may be the reason that we first became unhappy, but once we've grown up, it's no excuse for us to go on complaining. Our own attitudes sustain that needless suffering and it is ourselves that we must learn to forgive.

Our parents did whatever harm (and/or good) to us they may have done. There's no changing that. If we go on trying to be what we believe they wanted us to be, our nostalgia becomes a form of revenge. It is our way of showing them that they should have given us another chance and that we are preoccupied with how things might have been.

Acting as though we deserved their past mistreatment only makes us miss opportunities for happiness in the present. It may allow us to feel that we were loved when we were children, no matter how badly our parents may have treated us, but to maintain that illusion, we must go on feeling bad about ourselves.

We must learn to lose interest in our unhappy childhoods and forgive ourselves for having stayed stuck so long.

January 13

A SELF of our own seems like something we'd get automatically. But, then, why are many of us plagued with the confusing question, Who am I?

Some people lacked the opportunity to develop a cohesive core self in their earliest childhood, so when they grow up this question continues to absorb much of their energy. Their parents were likely too intrusive or too neglectful. Whether or not parents meant to do harm, children who receive inadequate parenting assume that they are inadequate children. So, they decide it's better to take cover, hide their real self, and fake one that pleases the adults on whom they depend.

Depending on the severity of the inadequacies and the degree to which we've become separated from our true selves, we may find ourselves faced with the task of developing a solid, real sense of self before we can get on with the next question, What do I want to do with my life?

We need to learn to be more like ourselves.

THE IDEA that we're having an identity crisis has become a popular explanation of times when we're simply uncertain or troubled. Sometimes this period in a person's life is a thinly veiled disguise for lack of initiative. Other times it seems like a good excuse for acting irresponsibly, such as taking drugs or having an affair.

Although being reckless isn't necessary or advisable, everyone needs to take time out to find a self. Unless you are willing to withdraw for a while, you won't be able to sort out who you really are from the person you're expected to be. During this time out, you will have to abandon many of the usual social standards, ignore the clamoring of those around you, and be still so you can hear your voice from within. Without this effort, your life will be spent trying to measure up to external standards. If you deny or never discover your true desires, you'll be left feeling empty and disconnected.

Once a great teacher was asked, "Where does God dwell?" He answered, "God dwells wherever people let Him in. But we can let Him in only where we really stand, in a place where we live a life that is truly our own."

If we are to find God, first we need to find ourselves.

January 15

MORE THAN a thousand years ago, the Chinese poet Li Po wrote:

> *Hard is the Journey,*
> *Hard is the Journey,*
> *So many turnings,*
> *And now where am I?*

It seems that people have always asked this question. Many have been tempted to accept answers offered by others. It is hard to resist the invitation to certainty, to making sense of it all by becoming one of the good guys, joining forces with the group.

How much heavier is the burden of making decisions on your own. How much lonelier is it to make your own way, to go on questioning everything, willing to forego tradition and others' approval.

Ask yourself, "What do I feel?" "What do I want?"—and then follow the stirrings from within. You risk being labeled an oddball or a maverick, but what's so awful about that?

Once we give up needing others' approval, we're free to do as we please.

A DEVOUTLY religious woman was once asked, "What if there were no God?" "Then," she declared, "nothing in the world would mean anything. I would probably kill myself." Her response raises the question, Even without meaning from any outside source, why not live? For many of us, the answer is that we are afraid of the absence of meaning in our lives because we are afraid of the freedom.

If we discovered that nothing outside ourselves would give us direction, then we would have to do whatever we wanted. Nothing would be certain and all would be possible. We would have to assume the responsibility for bringing meaning to our own lives. To make matters worse, we would realize that no one cares as much about us as we do about ourselves.

We can either be terrified and create false certainties to replace real ambiguities, or we can quit struggling against the tide, stop trying so hard to do what can't be done, and enjoy ourselves while we can.

What if there was no one to tell us what we shouldn't do?

January 17

MOST OF us spend a good portion of our lives as though we were performing on the stage of life. Surely there must be an audience out there somewhere! If no one is watching or listening, what would be the point of it all? Living in our own spotlight, we cannot see into the darkness of the empty house. Receiving no response, we assume we must be a flop. We think we need to try harder, to improve the show, to wait a bit longer. We wait in vain for the applause to come.

Or we can get off the stage and get a different view of what we're doing. How important is it to live our lives showing off so that others will admire us? How different our lives would be if we judged our performance in terms of how it feels to us, rather than how we imagine it looks to others? The question is not whether we should or shouldn't enjoy being appreciated but whether we want to spend our lives waiting for someone else to applaud.

The freedom to do as we please is one kind of power.

IN DOSTOEVSKY'S novella, *The Double*, the main character, Golyadkin Senior, is a chronic worrier. In his perfectionistic attempts to eliminate the contradictions within himself, he obsesses endlessly. To maintain the illusion that he is in control of his life, he dares not overlook any possibility that he may make a mistake. Ironically, it is just these anxious preoccupations that consume the energy he needs to cope with pressures of his personal life and career.

Pretending that things are better than they are, he makes his situation worse than it is, adding to his troubles by denying his dishonest efforts at getting along with other people. He stubbornly insists that he is on the verge of a new and better life.

Dostoevsky's story offers readers a reassuring, protective distance from the discomfort of identifying ourselves with this character who insists on deceiving himself.

Why suffer needlessly because you're not perfect when you can feel satisfied that you are good enough?

January 19

BECOMING OUR own selves should not be confused with being *selfish* or *self-centered*. We cannot become our selves without recognizing the ways we need to be with others and how we need to love other people. We can't test our values and feelings in a vacuum. We can't experience joy without reaching out.

Obsessing about ourselves is not enough. As the Hasids tell us, "You can rake the muck this way, rake the muck that way—it will always be muck. Have I sinned or have I not sinned? In the time I am brooding over it, I could be stringing pearls for the delight of heaven."

Worry if you must, but get on with living your life.

DETERMINED TO get rid of the Buddha, a treacherous demon unleashed an elephant to charge and destroy him. Just as the wild, raging beast was about to trample him, the Buddha raised his right hand with fingers held close together and palm open, facing the oncoming animal. The gesture of fearlessness completely subdued the dangerous animal. Once having faced the terrible threat of annihilation, the Compassionate Buddha cupped his other hand with its palm up, extending it as an offering of an open heart. This gesture of forgiveness restored the elephant's natural tranquility.

The Sanskrit word for these symbolic gestures is *mudra*. The Buddha's first mudra allowed him to face his fear. Having turned back terror, the Buddha was then free to confer on the elephant the second mudra of compassion that calmed the bewildered beast.

If we learn to raise our right hand against fear, we can extend the other in compassion.

January 21

HOW CAN we hope to find peace if we don't know what to look for? Ironically, we will probably learn most not from our greatest highs but from our deepest lows. These are the times when we have experienced a radically altered perspective about how we are living and we have felt dramatic shifts in our sense of time.

When a loved one was seriously ill or injured, for example, we may remember that our frantic plans for success or status simply dropped from our thoughts. While engrossed in concern for our loved one, we were temporarily freed from distractions and temptations that interfere with living centered on our selves. At least for the moment, we were almost wholly focused on those aspects of our lives that are most meaningful.

Personal peace is not uninterrupted happiness. One part of peace is attaining freedom from the needless suffering caused when we don't live our own lives in a way that includes attention to the misfortunes of others. Any experience that gives us even a brief sense of peace provides a clue to the larger serenity we seek.

Experiences of inner peace often arise in unexpected ways.

THEORIES ABOUT human experience rarely help us with our personal problems. Instead, we need to hear the stories of others so we can see "pictures in our head" and feel through our intuitive experience that we are not alone.

Sometimes just being alive feels like having no skin, just raw flesh—vulnerable, responsive, irritable, in constant danger. Those are the times when we need most to sense our place among other people, to hear their tale and know that it is ours as well. We need so badly to be sure that someone else can hear us, to receive their answering cry, to respond in kind.

In myths and folktales, it has always been clear that to flee a prophesy is to make it come true. That isn't meant as a fatalistic view of the future but as an understanding of what we are like. We cannot escape our selves without destroying ourselves. We cannot always face our fears entirely on our own. At times we need help, but whether alone or with support, if we do not face our fears we will never be free to be all we might become.

Whatever fear we suffer in solitude is also suffered by everyone else.

January 23

ANYONE CAN seek spiritual freedom. Some people seem able to attain this level of enlightenment, but no one can sustain it on a continuing basis. Spiritual freedom means that we live out who we are, doing exactly as we please, without any disparity between what we want to do and what we should be doing.

When you reach this state, you are past worrying about how well you are performing. Also, you're seemingly indifferent to obstacles and dangers. This naive fearlessness is very similar to the spontaneity of the child.

The central quality in this spontaneity is that you can trust yourself. No longer expecting to be certain or perfect, you give yourself over to being just who you are at the moment. Satisfied to be able to do what you can, you discover your ability to do far more than you could if you were still distracted by the question of how well you were doing.

Spiritual freedom comes when you devote your full attention to the task at hand.

GROWING UP often means facing the anguished isolation of no longer belonging as we wander in exile through a strange world that makes no sense. We all have to make our own separate way through an indifferent, unfamiliar landscape in which good is not necessarily rewarded and evil is not punished.

For some of us, it seems as though this is the way it has always been. So little protected and so badly hurt even as children, we dare not trust others. Distrust can protect us from being hurt again, but it precludes whatever loving closeness we might have with others, so the cost of such safety is even greater loneliness.

In order to enjoy those random moments of happiness, we must learn that we can survive emotionally, so we can afford to risk trusting and loving once more.

Revealing ourselves to others may mean taking our chances, but hiding out can be just as risky.

January 25

ONCE A young man believed that even though he struggled to claim the dark, hidden parts of himself, he couldn't accept the shadow side of himself. Then he had a telling dream.

Out in a very dark night, he had to walk slowly. Suddenly, feeling like a fool, he said to himself, "What are you doing out here without a flashlight?" Trying to find his way back home, he became aware of another presence—a dog, he thought.

Staying on the alert, he saw that the animal was not a dog but a wolf! At first he decided to kill the beast with his bare hands. Then, recognizing that was absurd, he realized that to survive, "I must make friends with this wolf!"

When he awoke, he understood that the wolf represented his savage soul, his secret shadow, and then the answer to his struggle was clear, "*The wolf is my own dark brother.* Instead of trying to overcome the terror of my hidden self, I must learn to own it, to make friends with it, so I can come to love the rest of myself."

Accepting our weaknesses frees our strengths.

LIFE WITHOUT illusions sometimes seems unbearable. When we hang on to illusion too long, we are trying to turn powerlessness into a virtue. Often, we whitewash our residual weakness, helplessness, and dependency with feigned humility.

By pretending that we are so frail, we make ourselves susceptible to anxiety and depression. By denying destructiveness in ourselves and others, we are turned toward unwitting complicity with evil. And clinging to the possibility of a perfect life robs us of our real power and sets us up for yet another inevitable disappointment.

Faking weakness takes much of our strength.

TOO OFTEN, as children, we were encouraged to try to be someone other than ourselves. It was demanded that we assume a character and live out a life-story written by someone else. The plot line was given and improvisations were seriously discouraged or completely unacceptable, and the direction was an oppressive form of close-quarter tyranny. Neurosis is, in part, the result of being miscast into a scenario plotted out in accord with somebody else's unfulfilled dreams and unfaced anxieties.

Most often the casting directors were our parents. From the start, some of us were cast as the stars our parents never were, and when we didn't fit the part, we were sources of disappointment. Some of us were cast as villains whose mere presence posed endless problems for starring parents.

As children we see no choice but to play these parts as best as we can, but when we get old enough to understand our options, many of us decide to be exactly the opposite of what our parents expected and so we end up playing another role. In the end defiance is no freer than compliance.

If you want to live your own life, you have to create your own story.

ALL OF us have thoughts and feelings that we don't approve of, and have done things we think we shouldn't have. Those who deny this must also deny their humanness of being part animal and part angel. Our paradoxical human nature is illustrated in the life of the infamous Marquis de Sade.

Sade was a dangerous criminal and scandalous pervert, yet he was a man with strong personal convictions, strongly opposing the artificial codes imposed by collective morality. It is interesting to observe that as he stepped beyond moral restraint, he was free to release his imagination to bring personal meaning to his experience. The issue is not whether Sade was right or wrong but only that what he did was freely chosen.

The particular value of his story lies in its ability to disturb us, to make us wonder. Are we passively conforming to social convention and group morality? If so, we're giving up any chance to lead original lives.

Until we experience how much is too much, how will we know how much is enough?

January 29

IT'S REALLY hard to come to terms with the idea that we will be accepted, liked, and loved because of who we are now, rather than because of what we have done in the past or what we will do in the future.

When we acknowledge that others' feelings for us do not depend on what we do, we begin to experience just how helpless we really are. If instead we hold on to the illusion that we can make someone love us—do something so someone will care—then we can keep on trying (no matter how unhappy that makes us). We can bribe or intimidate people, but once they get to know us, we can't control how they will feel about us of their own free will.

Once it's clear we can't get love by being good, or by being bad for that matter, we will simply have to settle for struggling along. Continuing honest efforts will have to be good enough to be considered doing our best.

Like it or not, we'll be loved for who we are, not who we were or who we want to be.

CHILDREN DO what they can to survive their long period of relative helplessness, but for some, the pressure to try to be someone other than who they are is overwhelming. In family settings where no one really cares enough to encourage them to find out who they might really be, there is no place to stand, no way to get perspective. To survive in this kind of situation, children must do what they can with the part they are given.

In the beginning, much of our suffering was the result of what was laid on us. But now, much of our misery is not the result of our problems but of our solutions. An honest appraisal of our situation may reveal that we've made ourselves into heroic exaggerations of what was actually required. Whether we've been playing at being super good or super bad, what began as a form of self-preservation has become a form of self-destruction. And now any kind of change is up to us.

How we live our adult lives is no longer any of our parents' business.

January 31

ALTHOUGH WE were born predisposed to certain personality characteristics, our development was affected more by our parents' own internal conflicts and unconscious fantasies. Beyond awareness, yours or theirs, some of your responses mirrored parts of their inner makeup that they couldn't bear to acknowledge, upsetting them beyond their emotional tolerance.

When you acted in ways that didn't trigger these angry emotional responses, your parents were nurturing, so you too accepted that aspect of yourself. When your responses reflected their unconscious, negative self-images, they reacted negatively. Soon you too disowned these reactions of yours as "not-me" and relegated them to the shadowy realm of your unconscious.

Unaccepted parts of ourselves are upsetting when we see them in others.

"WHAT IS the meaning of my life, or life in general?" In *Modern Man in Search of a Soul*, Carl Jung speaks eloquently of this and other "holy insecurities" we all must face if we want to take steps toward personal peace. To paraphrase Jung, when conscious life has lost its meaning or promise, we have no love, only sex; no faith, because we are afraid to grope in the dark; no hope, because we are disillusioned by the world and by life; and no understanding, because we have failed to read the meaning of our own existence.

Our suffering is incredible. We toss and turn in the night and drag ourselves through the day. Yet, pain is our only passageway to spiritual growth, because, as Jung says, human thought can't conceive a way to get what we need to live: faith, hope, love, and insight. These are gifts of grace that only come through experience. Jung quotes Holderlin, who said:

> *Danger itself*
> *Fosters the rescuing power.*

There is no nirvana without some sorrow.

February 2

ACTIONS ON the stage are meant to be relevant to the plot. But real life is more random—there are irrelevancies, repetitions, and boredom. But there is enough dramatic intensity to bring meaning to life, and we are freer when we move beyond the stylized, overly rehearsed reactions.

Cliched situations, stereotypical props, and phony backdrops accompany traditional scripts. But when we throw them away, what are we left with? What else can we do? In a world where we are free of parental direction, criticism, or applause, any action is permitted. And the only future that is sure is that we must face the consequences of our own acts, whatever they may be.

In a life that must be ad-libbed, we may be curious about what comes next and move beyond the role in which we've been cast. In other words, we can move out of the theater into the real world. Then the ending is unknown, but at least it's our own.

Willingness to risk can bring rewards we can't get otherwise.

THE MORE identified you are with your conscious personality, the less you will be aware of your shadow. You may unconsciously select other people to act out vicariously aspects of your own hidden self, or even encourage others to behave in ways that actually serve as your alter ego. If it meets the other person's needs, he or she may at the same time be using you as a reciprocal shadow. Think of how many couples live Laurel and Hardy lives, each a caricature of the other's disowned self.

If you believe that you have thoroughly purged the unacceptable parts of yourself, you may be one of those too-good-to-be-true people who believe that they cast no shadow. Though you can admit that no one is perfect, you find it difficult to recall a time when you were clearly in the wrong. If this is your posture, you are in a dangerous position. Whatever you've been unwilling or unable to face within yourself is likely to hit you in the face like a bucket of cold water.

One of our most dangerous mistakes is believing that we're always right.

February 4

NO ONE wants to think about the dreaded times when we will suffer great loss, but grief comes to everyone. In the Parable of the Mustard Seed, a young woman was so crazed about the death of her little son that she carried her dead child from house to house, demanding medicine for him. One sympathetic soul directed her to the monastery where the Compassionate Buddha taught.

"It is wise of you to have come," the Buddha said. "Here is what you must do. Go to each house in this city, one by one, and collect tiny grains of mustard seeds. But you must only take seeds from houses where no one has ever died."

Filled with gratitude, the mother set out immediately, asking at every door, "Is this a house where no one has died?" "Oh no," said each owner, "the dead from this house are beyond counting." On and on she went, but the answer was always the same—every family had been touched by death. Finally she understood: "There is no medicine for this but the acceptance of it."

Sometimes there is no cure except the knowing.

UNFORTUNATELY, SOME of us have learned to believe that we should feel ashamed any time we turn out to be less than the perfect child our parents expected us to be. As we grow older and realize that, unless we repair our damaged sense of self, we will never be able to meet that expectation, we simply cannot risk participating in situations where our personal inadequacies might be revealed. Feeling painfully, conspicuously shy, we withdraw from others, alone with our pain. Typically, we harbor the notion that other people are not as foolish as we are, or that they are tougher and more competent.

Our self-conscious preoccupation with being especially sensitive increases our sense of isolation, peculiarity, and loneliness. Lacking acceptance of ourselves, we're required to develop a protective style of acting timid most of the time and of avoiding letting others come to know us. The result is a partially unlived life.

One way or another, we are all misfits.

February 6

BY PLAYING the clown and the fool, Taoist teachers refused to put themselves above other men. They encouraged a fellow-feeling of fools among the community of ordinary people. Nothing was too sacred to be laughed at.

They were wise fools whose grand folly was an acceptance of everything just as it was, celebrating man's imperfections with laughter. In doing so, they encouraged the freedom for all of us to laugh at our follies.

An individual's failing is painful, but the shared frailties of all men are ultimately comic. So it is that one stutterer, or wheelchair-bound amputee, or one addict alone is tragic, but together they can be free for a moment to laugh at their own situation. As Zen wisdom tells us, this laughter is itself a form of reverence. It is the laughter of acceptance, and appreciation, and wonder.

God grant me the laughter. —AA slogan

THERE IS no shame in being ignorant, but if we want to learn something we don't yet know, like Socrates, we must first admit, "I only know that I know not."

When someone speaks about something you don't understand, swallow your pride and ask to be instructed. Some people may add to your discomfort by replying, "I can't believe that you don't know that," but you may be surprised to find that many others will admire your openness and be happy to share their knowledge with you.

You may be tempted to try to gloss over your ignorance, or to hide it behind some unfounded opinion. But it is then that you'd be wise to remember the folk wisdom of Josh Billings: "It ain't what a man don't know that makes him a fool, but what he does know that ain't so."

Ignorance won't hurt anything, unless we aren't willing to acknowledge it.

February 8

BELIEVING THAT this is the best of all possible worlds is an overly optimistic Pollyanna attitude, but believing that things usually turn out bad is paranoid and just as naive. Both the paranoid and the Pollyanna are preoccupied with what is going on outside themselves. Focusing on what others do and how things turn out divert attention from unacceptable aspects of their own inner lives.

Paranoids attribute to others characteristics they can't accept in themselves. Pollyannas demand a caring, protective world, implying they deserve a life in which everything always works out for the best.

Each extreme is an oversimplified view of life's ambiguities. One view is too bad to be real and the other is too good to be true. And both are ways to rationalize your way out of taking care of yourself.

Making the best of what we've got is the best choice we can make.

THE THRESHOLD of each new stage of life involves a crisis. Also, there are almost daily small losses that seem part of growing up, and that recur throughout our lives.

When the important transitions occur, they seem too painful to endure without the protection of a temporary hedge. For example, when a loved one dies, the stages of grief—the initial numbing shock and the denial—help the mourner from being consumed by sorrow. When crises come too early, or come on us too savagely, or must be faced in an atmosphere of emotional hypocrisy, the needed protection of pretending may become an enduring lifestyle.

If we stay stuck in perpetual denial, we are handicapped with a naive understanding of what will bring happiness—a belief that causes us unnecessary disappointment and exaggerated suffering. Denial of real danger makes it easier to get hurt.

The temporary protection of pretending must be exchanged for the enduring protection of our understanding life as it is.

February 10

IT IS possible to be sane and yet to imagine that you are crazy. But it's also possible to be crazy without knowing it. There are times when you believe you are the only one who is sane, and even those times may turn out to be the ones when you are really crazy.

Some dilemmas seem unresolvable: What is real and what is unreal? Who is sane and who is insane? When am I doing the right thing and when the wrong?

Who knows? When there is no hope of finding an answer, the only release is in allowing yourself to lose interest in the search. When you find yourself at peace, you will realize that it's only because you forgot the question.

Sometimes the only answer is to give up trying to find the answer.

IN HASIDISM, a Jewish mystical movement of the eighteenth and nineteenth centuries, the zaddik was the spiritual leader who served as rabbi to his community. Often he answered questions by telling stories or sharing his own experiences.

The zaddik was a helper who would extend his hand to followers, and if the followers would take it, he would guide them until they were able to find their way alone. Yet, he did not relieve them of the responsibility of doing for themselves whatever they had grown strong enough to do. And, at no time did he free people from the burden of what they must do for themselves. As one rabbi explained, "What you don't get by your own work, you don't have."

No one else can find your higher power for you.

February 12

WHEN WE are scared and uncertain, we're most vulnerable to believing that someone somewhere must be smart enough to know what's best for us and will be strong enough to come to our rescue. This happens to all of us at times.

Unfortunately, some people spend their lives waiting to be rescued. Stubbornly insisting on trusting almost anyone's judgment instead of their own, the dependent seekers find themselves let down, exploited, and betrayed again and again. Still the search goes on for someone who is sufficiently wise and kind to be trusted with responsibility. The repeated disappointments hurt, but the prospect of being on their own seems too overwhelming. They believe that having to take care of themselves would turn out even worse.

One person thinks, "I was never properly cared for, so how would I know how?" Another thinks, "I was always taken care of, so I never learned how." In reality, they already are on their own. Unfortunately, they aren't consciously aware of how they are choosing to run their lives.

We each must trust ourselves to make our own choices.

AT PARTICULAR points along the way, a soul-searching spiritual journey may follow different paths. Everything works. Nothing works. Unwittingly we stumble onto a particular path. Once we recognize where we are, we must consciously choose to do what we are already doing. We will follow that path until it seems to go nowhere, then wander in despair for a time until we blunder onto another. Again, it is time to accept responsibility without blame for this phase in our journey.

Often we don't deliberately make the significant decision. Instead, we come to realize that somewhere along the way the decision has already been made. Then, we need to surrender and responsibly accept the choice as our own.

In every important aspect of our lives, we will discover attitudes in ourselves we weren't aware of and find ourselves in situations that only later we realize we chose ourselves.

Giving up blaming others for our own decisions is a big step.

February 14

RILKE WRITES, "Love is not learned," and neither is it chosen. We cannot decide whether or not to love someone. The feelings arise or they do not. Our only alternatives are to accept them or to try to ignore them, to act in accordance with our caring or to avoid further contact with someone who begins to matter to us.

If we've been abused or abandoned by people we cared about too many times in the past, we are likely to play it safe. We cannot decide never to love again, but we can be more careful about whom we entrust with our affection—it's important to be careful, but not too careful.

We have to discover the breakpoint between cowardice and recklessness, between taking worthwhile risks and missing opportunities for better relationships than we've ever had before. There's no hope for receiving love that can be trusted unless we are willing to take chances. Risk getting hurt once more, or settle for life without a love that is fulfilled.

We cannot love without the willingness to risk getting hurt.

PERSONAL POWER doesn't come from trying to control external events and other people. A person cannot do what cannot be done. Life is not a matter to be managed. We have little influence on its outcome. Our only impact is on how we live it.

We didn't ask for the responsibility of taking charge of ourselves, but it's the only power to which we're entitled. And to avoid the pitfalls we must recognize the corrupting temptations raised by both dominance and submission.

While power over others may sound desirable at times, real power is self-confidence and self-direction. These feelings of being in charge of our lives allow us the freedom to do as we please.

Once we accept the responsibility of taking charge of our own lives, we lose interest in controlling the lives of others.

IMAGINATION IS the heartland of human experience, not simply the quality of thought of children, madmen, and fools. It is not merely a passing state of mind. Along with memory, imagination is the mind.

Through the power of our minds, we form concepts that bring order to otherwise random events in ways that allow us to make our way through this life, guided by expectations colored by fear or hope. There is a time for hope and a time for fear. Bringing the same attitude to every situation is not a sign of character, but rather an indication of a character disorder.

Out of fear, we act to avoid something, or in hope, we want to bring about some positive result. In either case, we intend some particular outcome. No matter what we choose to do or not to do, what happens as a result is our responsibility.

We may tell ourselves that we can't help what we do, but responsibility for our actions and attitudes is ours nonetheless.

MEDITATION AIMS at liberating by developing mastery over the mind. It begins with concentration, but it isn't possible to concentrate without straying. There are many possible distractions, such as thinking of the past, worrying about the future. Even when you seem to be focused on the present, self-consciousness can be a distraction.

Comparisons are always deadly, whether they pivot around how you are the same or different from another person, or even how different you are now than you were or will be. The goal is to have your whole being concentrated in what you are doing at the moment. As Saint Anthony said, "The prayer of the monk is not perfect until he no longer realizes himself or the fact that he is praying."

We can't force our minds to be patient and stay calm. Instead we must learn to witness discomforting interruptions, and when distraction comes, Lawrence LeShan suggests we gently say to ourselves, "Oh, that's where I am. Now back to work." Instead of resistance, we simply go back to one and begin again.

If you want to play freely, stop keeping score.

TO COPE with life's contradictions, we must anticipate change. If we're unprepared for the transitions, we miss the opportunities they can provide.

At the crossroads of contradictions, people who remain stubborn and opposed to inevitable change may find it useful to try the left-handed path of tantra yoga. In dealing with difficult attitudes, tantra teaches: When you can't give up, give in! Continue doing what you do. As time passes, the contradictions will grow congruent.

Tantric practices sound simple, but they are not easy. The central theme is that like cures like. When we surrender to our weaknesses, stumbling blocks can be turned into stepping stones. Poison is an antidote to poison. This medieval wisdom evolved as a way of instructing those who could not say "no" to temptation.

If you are naturally resistant, then you feel like doing the opposite of whatever you're told. When you're told to keep doing what you're already doing, if you stop, you're giving up the behavior; if you don't stop, you're giving in and no longer resisting. Either way, you win.

Stubbornness is a source of strength waiting to be freed.

A STORY in Hindu mythology tells of Krishna dancing with many women in a way that expressed emotion overflowing from a full heart. If we learn what this tale has to teach, it frees us from the assumption that there is only so much love to go around.

In the story, Krishna responds to a question about love, explaining that there are those who love expecting to receive love in return, selfishly seeking their own happiness. When people pair in this way, they are using each other, rather than simply loving. Then there are those who love though there is no love given in return; as mates, these people are kind and compassionate caretakers who can be depended on to be good friends. A third type is incapable of returning the love offered and therefore is self-satisfied, distant, and indifferent.

Krishna's own alternative was to willingly devote himself entirely to each one he loved, and invite each to be completely dedicated to him.

The more we love one person, the more we can love others as well.

IN ORDER to grow physically, we have to take risks. If we want to learn to walk, we must be willing to fall. To grow spiritually, we must also risk and sacrifice. The simple, elusive truth must be learned again and again: You cannot hope to find your self unless you are first willing to lose yourself.

For as long as you can remember, your self-image has been highly selective both in what it includes and excludes. To grow you must be open to ideas that previously were unthinkable. If you will allow yourself to think and act more freely, your relationships with others will change. The ones that don't last may not have been worthwhile.

There are many opportunities for personal growth. We can seek them deliberately by trying therapy or meditation. But sometimes the chance is thrust upon us by a painfully stressful situation. Any experience that unsettles our ordinary sense of reality or challenges our unexamined identity offers access to the rest of the self.

Pain and disruption are the gateways to spiritual growth, but stepping across the threshold is up to you.

THE MORE you accept yourself the better you feel. It isn't as easy as it sounds, but just trying to get used to your flaws and frailties relieves the tension. You don't need the false modesty of declaring that "Nobody's perfect" and "Everybody makes mistakes." An honest look at yourself will provide modesty enough.

When you give up your perfectionistic ideals, you actually increase your self-acceptance and restore your self-esteem. By reducing your own demands of who you should be, you can live more comfortably with who and what you are. Paradoxically, it is this acceptance of what is that increases your chances of becoming all you possibly can. Simply scaling down your image to life-size eases tensions, spares you from blaming yourself, and adds to the pleasure you can have from everyday life.

Just scaling down our arrogance makes us feel better about ourselves.

February 22

To SOME degree, everyone has a divided personality. Even those who grew up in near-optimal circumstances find reasons to disavow some parts of their selves. However, the protection of this disowning causes its own kind of pain. For all of us, reclaiming our unacceptable aspects helps put our selves back together into a happier whole.

Before we can do this, we need to be aware of what it feels like to have a self of our own. The boundary between self and not-self is a crucial experience. Most of the time we are not "self-conscious" of the psychological or the physical "me" until the boundaries of one or the other is challenged. When we are threatened with being violated physically or emotionally, our boundaries become painfully clear, if only on an intuitive level.

When your gut-level says, "Hey, you can't do that to me!" it's a clear signal that what you feel a need to defend is a part of yourself.

To find a self of your own, you have to discover where you begin and other people end.

THERE IS no way to be certain what we really are. Our self-concept is an image composed of both what we hope and what we fear we might be. Most of us are tempted to believe that our public self is a true representation of who we really are.

From the very beginning, we each must learn to accommodate or die. Emotional survival is largely a matter of maintaining self-esteem. If we've had to struggle too hard for this survival, we're likely to focus on the less desirable self we've imagined, primarily believing what we fear is true about us. Then it's most useful to remember that, like our idealized self-image, our worst fears are also caricatures created in our imaginations.

Unless you feel good enough about yourself, life doesn't seem worth living. You could give up trying because your limits are causing you pain. Or, you might try to imagine that you are no better or worse than anyone else, and then decide to do the best you can.

Freedom lies in having no choice but to be who you already are.

February 24

WHAT CAN we hope to be for one another in this frightening, exciting world in which we are both trapped and free? We need to come to know each other, for there is little else that has real meaning. We must learn what it is we have to give, and what we may hope to receive.

What we can hope to get—and hope to give—is the strength and comfort of knowing there are others who feel what we feel, struggle as we struggle, who mourn their losses and survive. Grateful for the gifts of caring companions, we value most the courage we get from their support so we can be our own sort of person.

Being on your own doesn't mean being all alone.

TO SOME extent, we all still live in the darkness of our own unfinished past. The refusal to mourn the disappointments and losses of childhood (as well as other ages and stages of our lives), to bury them once and for all, condemns us to live in their shadows.

Genuine grief is the sobbing and wailing that express the acceptance of our helplessness to do anything about our loss. If instead we complain, insist that this cannot be, or demand to be compensated for our pain, then we are forever stuck with trying to bring back what can't possibly be redeemed. If we refuse to accept that we cannot change our past misfortunes, we will also lose the warm, loved feelings of past joys. Future pleasures will taste bittersweet if their flavor is spoiled by the ashes of the past.

We must allow ourselves to feel sad and helpless, and then we must go on.

February 26

ZEN BUDDHISM instructs that reflection about life must not be confused with life itself. Life is to live. So it is said, if one points his finger at the moon, it would be a great mistake for another to stare at the finger and believe he knows the moon.

Zen masters sometimes teach by using puzzling problems called koans. For example, "What is the sound of one hand clapping," or "Show me your original face before you were born." A disciple may spend months or years trying to solve the problem until it occurs to him that the only "solution" is to give up trying to understand because there is nothing to be understood. In that instant of awakening, there is no problem and so he can respond spontaneously.

The disciple already knows all there is to know, but he does not trust his spontaneous perception of the world. By insisting there must be more to it, some secret to be discovered, he creates a problem much like the survival problem of a man who has his hands clutched tightly around his own throat.

We create some problems by seeking their solution.

CHILDREN WHO grow up in families that are emotionally unsafe or insufficiently supportive develop ways of coping. These defensive attitudes make sense at the time and are required for the child's emotional survival. For example, children of demanding parents may become overly compliant, whereas those of erratic parents make distrustful vigilance a first priority.

Unfortunately, some of these children continue this skewed outlook into adulthood. As grown-ups, they act as though the world was the same as the home in which they grew up. What was once a sane, appropriate response to their surroundings becomes a crazy, unwarranted reenactment of attitudes and behavior that no longer are necessary.

Neurosis is continuing to act as if we were coping with the problems of childhood, when growing up has changed where we stand in our world.

THE TRADITION of early spiritual leaders teaches that self-conscious spirituality is no spirituality at all. One story tells of a certain monk, a solitary celibate, who met some nuns on the road and fled at the sight of them. The abbess spoke to him wisely, saying, "If you were a true solitary monk, you wouldn't have looked close enough to see that we were women."

The teachers also warned that it is easy to be tempted to take pride in one's humility. Another story tells how a young brother took the habit and announced, "I am going to be a solitary." But when the older men heard him, they came to his cell and threw him out, making him go to the cells of each brother saying, "Forgive me, for I am no solitary, but have only now tried to become a monk."

Self-conscious spirituality and prideful humility are contradictions in terms for any era's pilgrims who hope to find a path to personal peace.

If we pay attention to personal peace, we interrupt our spiritual quest.

NO MATTER how hard we try to please others, there will still be people who don't like us. And no matter how much we ignore the expectations of others, some people will care about us anyway.

Heywood Broun wrote, "The man who has cured himself of B.O. and halitosis, has learned French to surprise the waiter, and the saxophone to amuse the company, may find that people still avoid him because they do not like him."

Whether or not we will be liked is one of the uncertainties we just have to live with. We each have the right to be our own singular self and to do and say things in our own peculiar way. The only restriction is that what we do must not limit others' freedom to do the same.

If you spend your life trying to be the person everyone likes, you waste the person you are.

March 1

HOW DO I find a self of my own? What is the purpose of my life? Whether moved by pain, drawn by longing, or inspired by hope, we search for answers, but what we find are more questions. These uncertainties are universal and yet their resolution is unique and personal.

Throughout time, people have set out on spiritual pilgrimages, on quests for personal meaning and peace. Often these journeys begin because of some kind of crisis. This isn't really surprising, because when we're happy and comfortable, we want things to remain the same, but when we're unsettled, we seek change.

As much as we may hope for help with the struggle, we must learn the most important lessons on our own. As a Zen master once said to a student, "If I did not make you fight in every way possible in order to find the meaning, you would lose every chance of discovering yourself."

To find what peace is possible, we must make our own pilgrimage. Along the way we must learn what we can and accept what we must. The important thing is to begin.

As we make our way on the pilgrimage that is our life, however well we may prepare, the moment belongs to God.

DISAPPOINTMENTS AND other sorts of misfortunes happen to everyone. As Harold Kushner tells us, sometimes bad things happen to good people, and conversely, sometimes bad people get fortunate breaks.

Regardless of the luck you have, if you want to feel worthwhile, you have to act decently. Still, it won't do any good to stand around waiting for rewards. Nobody's keeping score. As John H. Holmes wrote in *A Sensible Man's View of Religion*, "The universe is not hostile, nor yet is it friendly. It is simply indifferent." Doing good is its own reward. Also, an evil-doer is not necessarily punished for sinning, but is punished by doing wrong.

We must learn not to take everything personally.

March 3

ROBERT FROST wrote, "Home is the place where, when you have to go there, they have to let you in." Whether or not that was true of the home we grew up in, we all need a place where it's safe to be ourselves.

We all have our own peculiarities and we're all a little weird at times. That's why we need a place to drop our guard without feeling afraid of being ostracized for being as crazy as we naturally are. A nurturing family is one where members recognize each other's frailties and accept them, even though they can be a bother.

For those not lucky enough to be born into this kind of family, authors Pamela Ryan and Doris Jasinek suggest focusing on those around you who are willing to be part of a mutually caring support group. They propose that, whether related or not, "A family is a circle of people who love you."

It's never too late to build a home of your own.

LIFE ISN'T all you want, but it's all you get. The more you care about someone or something, the more you miss it when it's gone. Yet, unless we love passionately and grieve with proportionate intensity, we knowingly limit our possibilities for joy.

A prisoner clings to the small, barred window of his cell, desperately trying to see the little piece of sky visible to him. Ironically, if only he could let go long enough to turn around, cross the cell, and try the door, he might find that it has been unlocked all the time he was peering through the bars of his window. If so, he would be free to escape and walk freely under the vast openness of the sky.

Why cling desperately to what little you have when letting go might free you to have so much more?

March 5

WHEN WE want to know our place in another person's heart, we listen carefully to what they say to us and how they say it. But, sometimes, we can be fooled by both their words and their tone of voice.

It helps to have an overall understanding of how that particular person experiences relationships and other events. An equivalent overview of ourselves is even more important.

Some of us are thinking types, whereas others are feeling types. When a thinker says, "I love you," it may only be the expression of an idea in his or her head. And if a feeler expresses an opinion, it may amount to no more than an emotional reaction that has not been thought out.

The word is not the thing and the map is not the territory.

THERE ARE times when we feel *lonesome*. It is a longing for companionship, particularly of the people we care about. Missing them is easily remedied by being with them once more.

But, feeling *lonely* is another matter. Loneliness is an inescapable aspect of being human; it is an awareness of our separateness. Paul Tillich wrote, "Loneliness can be conquered only by those who can bear solitude." If we feel sufficiently at home with ourselves, even the company of others feels intrusive at times.

Ironically, the most excruciating experience of loneliness comes when we are in the company of, but out of contact with, our most intimate partners. If you want to make yourself really lonely, get married and depend on your mate to make your life meaningful.

If two people are to be able to fully enjoy being together, they must first learn the rewards of being alone.

March 7

BRECHT TELLS of an old man who lived in a village that was occupied by the Nazis. The storm trooper who took over his cottage ordered the old man to make his bed, shine his boots, and cook his meals. But when the oppressor demanded that he agree to serve him, the old man would not answer.

For two years, he obediently served the invader, but all the while he remained silent. At last, the Allies retook the village. Just as they were dragging the storm trooper off to the prisoner-of-war camp, the old man took a deep breath and finally answered the question, "No!"

Giving in is not the same as giving up.

WE ARE free to do as we please as long as we are willing to take responsibility for the consequences of our actions. An unhappy childhood causes a person's life to start out on the wrong foot.

As adults, we may continue to act as if we were still children in the home where we were raised. Perhaps there should be a statute of limitations on the causes of later misbehavior.

When we think of ourselves as neurotic, we absolve ourselves of responsibility for inappropriate actions and attitudes by excusing them as irrational and beyond our control. Once we understand the intent of our "symptomatic" way of living, we recognize what we do as constricted, controlling, or at times, even cruel.

We can go on acting like fools or fiends, but we can no longer act as if we have a note from our doctor excusing us as ill.

Neurosis is a way of behaving badly without feeling that we are to blame.

March 9

SOME OF us see other people as "having it all to-gether." Because they display an air of confidence when they take risks, we assume that they know all the answers.

Often, it turns out that people who live freely, without seeming to worry a great deal about the outcome of their actions, are only wiser than the rest of us. They know that despite the many unresolvable uncertainties, an unlived life is not worth examining.

What do we know for sure . . . anyway?

ASKING, "ARE we having fun yet?" is a sardonic way of saying, "I think I'm supposed to be having fun, but I'm not." What, then, do you propose to do about it, since happiness cannot be pursued directly?

Living our lives is like participating in an interesting conversation or satisfying lovemaking. If we set out to achieve a preplanned result, we will miss out on much of the fun that comes from immersing ourselves in the activity. In both cases, pleasure arises out of the exploring of possibilities with our partner, losing ourselves in the experience, and enjoying how well it goes and how long it lasts. Coming to a stunning conclusion is simply the delightful outcome produced by devoting ourselves to the ongoing exchange of spontaneous responses.

Happiness is a by-product of the process of devoting yourself fully to something else that is happening.

March 11

SOME PEOPLE have had their hearts broken so early or so often that fear and despair make them feel that they don't know how to love. This may be partially true if they've learned from unhappy or inappropriate role models in their lives.

Aldous Huxley wrote, "There isn't any formula or method. You learn to love by loving—by paying attention and doing what one thereby discovers has to be done." His seemingly radical statement asserts that learning to love comes naturally, if nothing gets in the way to distract us and we love in our own personal way.

There is nothing to learn that we do not already know. However, we may need to work on getting over the traumatic residue of a painful past that gets in the way of a pleasure-filled future. Now we must heal long-ago heartbreaks so that we can unlearn the ways we acquired to avoid loving again.

When it comes to learning to love, we already know all we need to.

SOME PEOPLE imagine that when life isn't all good, it is all bad. They split everything into polar opposites that make the mixed bag of everyday living a needlessly difficult experience. For instance, when a few difficult minutes interrupt their routine, they label the whole day as a total loss and perpetuate that notion, feeling sorry for themselves. Then something else happens, a compliment on their appearance or an invitation to go out, and their emotions soar as high as they had been low just moments before.

The price they pay for riding this emotional roller coaster is that whenever they aren't feeling wonderful, they feel terrible. Often they behave like the "little girl who had a little curl right in the middle of her forehead": When they feel good, they treat other people well, but when they don't, they act horrid.

We have to accept that even though at times we may feel troubled, often this imperfect, changing life is all that we have.

March 13

FOR THE most part, judging our lot by comparing it with how others are doing is an exercise in futility. When we have no shoes and invoke the image of others who have no feet, we still remain shoeless.

If we are doing all right, and envy others who have it better, we ignore whatever troubles they may be suffering and miss out on enjoying what we do have. The best way for deciding how we're doing is to pay attention to what our situation feels like at the moment.

Whether what you have is better or worse than what someone else has is irrelevant.

SOME PEOPLE assume that when a couple argues, their relationship is in jeopardy. Paradoxically, it is often when couples don't argue that one partner is startled to learn that the other has decided to leave. "How could that be?" the abandoned one wonders. "We never said a cross word to each other."

It's hard enough to live with the conflict within ourselves. How much more difficult is it to live with someone else without expressing the dissatisfaction with our differences, arguing them out whenever possible, and negotiating when we cannot convince the other that our way is best?

A relationship untested by open conflict cannot be trusted. Beneath the surface calm of seeming accord is the simmering turbulence of uncertainty about whether the relationship would last if we were open about unstated conflicts.

Anyone worth living with is worth fighting with.

MANY PEOPLE seem to suffer the fear of rejection. To avoid the disapproval of others, they limit how much of themselves they allow to be seen.

Ironically, many of these same people are also uncomfortable when anything about them evokes approval. It is as if they'd rather simply go unnoticed.

Often, the covert reason for this is a hidden fear of acceptance. If something they do is met with appreciation, they become afraid that, from then on, they will have to perform at least as well all of the time, and that even more might be expected of them.

The underlying need to be perfect encourages both a sense of inadequacy and a reluctance to do as well as we can.

ON THOSE unfortunate occasions when we believe that we have contributed to making a mess, most of us have learned to ask ourselves, "What did I do wrong?" We try to figure out what our part has been so that we won't make the same mistake next time. Often learning from past experience is a useful way to limit needless suffering in the future.

Oddly enough, we commonly put more emphasis on the prevention of needless suffering than on the facilitation of potential joy. When things work out well, false modesty keeps us from asking ourselves what we did to bring about our own happiness. More often, we feel lucky about getting a break for once. Frequently, the closest we get to claiming credit is by saying, "Well, I must have done something right!"

It serves us well to pay careful attention to those times when we do something right.

WE ARE our secrets. Although our innermost self-worth pivots on what remains private, often when we do a good deed, we announce it publicly and seek immediate applause. If instead, we do something petty or mean, we are tempted to hide it from others, and, if we can, to deny it even to ourselves. This kind of spiritual accounting results in an inner bankruptcy of self-esteem overlaid by a superficial but very vulnerable image of success in the eyes of others.

Note what happens when you try reversing the strategy. First admit to the weaknesses, errors, and follies that might make others see you as unworthy. At the same time that you divest yourself of sinful secrets, begin trying to hide the charities, virtues, and good deeds you once advertised. You can then depend on a store of hidden assets to bolster your self-respect when things are going badly.

Try to do right and leave the results to God.

SOME CHILDREN were raised without enough parental validation of who they were and what they were worth. When these neglected youngsters grow up, they usually don't feel entitled to other people's recognition of either the existence or the value of their identity.

As if trying to ransom back their stolen identities, they try hard to please others so that they'll validate their uncertain worth. Paradoxically, they are more likely to expect and accept criticism than appreciation in return, and they pay an exorbitant price of unnecessary accommodation and deference. Ironically, when people betray themselves in these needlessly degrading ways, they do not ransom back who they are. They become unwitting accomplices in the repetition of the original theft.

Once you're a grown-up, no one can kidnap your soul unless you act as an accomplice.

March 19

OFTEN LIFE seems so painfully ambiguous that we will grasp at anything that offers the illusion of identity, certainty, and stability. When we do not feel entitled to what we need, some of us settle for accepting whatever we can get from others, and in doing this, we allow them to define our identities and our situations.

Better to be a jerk, a wimp, or a fool than to not know what we are, or worse yet, to be a nobody. But if, in our own minds, we are not entitled to acceptance or have not earned rewards in return for our efforts because of who we are, then everything is given and so everything can be taken away.

What we give ourselves sometimes serves us better than what we get from others.

THERE ARE many different ways to add to feeling good about who you are. You can choose a task and enjoy accomplishing it. Mastery of new skills adds to self-confidence, but difficulty with new challenges may diminish sense of worth if your self-esteem depends on having power.

You can outdo someone else, but you won't win every contest. The next time you try, you may end up feeling as bad about losing as you felt good about winning. That's because, unfortunately, no matter what you do, some people will disapprove. If you look to others to see how you should feel about yourself, popularity polls will turn your sense of self-esteem into a roller-coaster ride.

However, if you listen to yourself and do whatever you believe is good, then you will feel good about yourself. Even if no one else agrees with you, you'll still come out ahead because you will have all the votes you need.

God and one person constitute a majority.

March 21

SOME PEOPLE act as though there is only a limited amount of love to go around. When someone else is loved, they envy and resent the tenderness the other receives. It's as if that caring leaves less love available for others. Also, based on the same belief, people are stingy about offering others the love they have in their own hearts.

This kind of faulty thinking leads people to operate in an emotional economy of assumed scarcity. To get and to give the love you want, you need to understand that when you love, your heart expands to allow you to love more. Similarly, when someone else is loved, the result is a sense of abundant caring with more affection available to you and to everyone else who is open to receiving it.

The more love you give, the more you have left to give.

HOW ARE we to know what is real and freely chosen, what is here and now? Even if everyone else believes we should act in a particular way, does conscience by committee result in right living?

Without any possibility of being certain of our assessments, we must learn to do the best we can and to find it sufficient. And when we have done all that we can, we must learn to give up and to forgive ourselves for not having been able to do more.

The option of lonely independence versus self-sacrificing conformity is only one of the polarities that we must face on our own with only the higher power within each of us as a guide.

Too often we form negative attachments rather than face the fear of being alone.

March 23

UP TO a certain age, there are ways in which young children make marvelous role models. They are totally honest and always spontaneous. They express their feelings openly, cry out when they feel frustrated, and are perfectly satisfied when their needs are met. When an upsetting experience has passed, they are completely happy once again. Very young children carry no grudges.

Just when we could relearn so much from them, we insist on teaching them to behave themselves. They soon learn to hide their true feelings, to manipulate to get what they want, and to harbor resentments where once they were able to live fully in each moment.

Some of this civilizing is necessary for the child to learn to deal with the socialized adult world, but an exorbitant price can be paid in exchanging openness for guile, and spontaneity for calculated, mannered behavior.

We can stop acting childish by allowing ourselves to be childlike.

WE ARE tempted to avoid situations that we expect will turn out unpleasant. When we are caught up in this threshold anxiety, we procrastinate. Often that simply makes it more difficult to take on whatever actions make us apprehensive.

Whenever we successfully avoid whatever it is we dread and the terrible outcome we expect does not occur, we miss the opportunity to discover that we could have gone ahead anyway. Avoidant behavior encourages us to continue avoiding.

We may try to tell ourselves that first we'll work out our anxiety and then we'll take action. It's like a person who's afraid of the water trying to learn to swim by reading an instruction book. The only way to understand some of the ways we behave is by trying to change them.

Obsessing is a poor substitute for action.

March 25

THERE ARE no words sufficient to express deeply felt love. We can tell our beloved what we value about them most, but who knows why we love one person who has these qualities, and only like and admire another.

Love is a stroke of grace. We may know how to please someone else, but we can't make anyone love us. We know we love when having the other person in our lives makes us happy to be alive.

When we are willing to express our love openly, we allow ourselves to feel our caring more deeply. Ironically, it is just as these times when we declare our devotion that we are most vulnerable to being hurt. To make matters more complicated, it's not enough to say, "I love you," only once and then assume the matter is settled once and for all.

Love is fragile. It requires repeated confirmation in word and deed. How we treat our beloved is more important than our verbal reassurances, but we need to repeat the words nonetheless. Love needs renewal again and again.

Seize every opportunity to say "I love you."

FROM TIME to time, even the most loving couples have painful arguments. Some of this discord begins when one partner's feelings are hurt by something the other has said or done.

Sometimes the injured party withdraws, leaving the other feeling bewildered and abandoned. Other times, the one who first felt attacked counters by fighting back. Frequently, these exchanges escalate into a contest of wills about who has been the more offensive.

"I can't believe you'd do anything that bad."

"You do things that are even worse!"

Some arguing is necessary and can be productive in working out ways to live together more comfortably, but not the sort of retorts and critical remarks that are intended to hurt.

A relationship doesn't get better by one partner making the other feel bad.

REMEMBER TIMES you had thoughts or feelings so foreign or bizarre that you felt the need to immediately reassure yourself by disowning them? Wherever that thought came from, certainly it was not the real you! You found yourself saying, "What a crazy idea!" or "What an awful way for anyone to feel! That's not like me at all." You dismissed your uneasiness by thinking of the familiar reasonable and consistent everyday image of who you are.

There have been times when another side of you has taken over so completely that, at least briefly, it was as if you were someone else. How could you have acted the way you did? Even now, it's uncomfortable just remembering how you behaved. The only way you've lived with the memory is by insisting that it was not you: "I was not myself that day," or "I must have been out of my mind."

Those times when your shadow side threatens to take over, you may feel as though you are "coming apart" or "going to pieces." But at that moment, even temporary insanity seems like a more acceptable option than acknowledging some terrible aspect of who you really are.

When dealing with your shadow side, either you get it or it gets you.

WHEN YOUNGSTERS, learning to get along with a world they can't control, comply with parental or social values automatically and without question, they become temporary captives of standards set by other people. Later, as adolescents, most attempt to establish their personal identity simply by assuming a defiant attitude, confusing rebellion with liberty.

It takes a while to learn that trying to define who you are by arbitrarily refusing to do what is expected attaches you to ethics that aren't truly your own just as much as obedient conformity does.

Some residue of these developmental phases remain active issues for many of us in later life. As adults, there are times when we must say "No" or betray our personal integrity. Other situations require that we say "Yes" to standards suggested by others because they feel right to us.

Compliance can keep us from being free, but so can rebellion.

March 29

SOME PEOPLE undertake a spiritual search much like children watching a colorful but somewhat frantic three-ring circus. There is too much to take in at once. The inner development of these overstimulated seekers is too distracted by each new option to allow them the growth that comes of immersing themselves in a single spiritual path. They are perennial initiates whose attention wanders from one trendy mystical way to the next. Their spiritual seeking amounts to membership in a guru-of-the-month club.

This is not to say that seekers should simply pick the first path they find and dedicate their lives to holding the course. We may choose a path, work at it for a while, and if we find that it doesn't suit our spiritual temperament, we would be wise to move on. Giving up on one way to try another may also make sense when, no matter what we attempt, we cannot get past remaining stuck at a certain point.

The problem may be less the path we choose than the way we travel it.

WHETHER WE have or don't have power, what means the most is what we do with it or don't do without it. When you have power, you usually feel important and pleased that you can get things others don't have. Unfortunately, you may also feel that people who aren't as powerful don't matter as much as you do.

It is also tempting to become captivated by the experience of power. It's a heady feeling that may cause you to violate your own beliefs about how you should treat other people. You are likely to be arrogant, demanding, or inconsiderate.

The absence of power also corrupts. When you are on the powerless side of a relationship, you are just as tempted to violate your beliefs. You may feel reduced to being subversive, dishonest, and downright sneaky.

We must learn to take responsibility for both our power and our helplessness.

March 31

FOR THE sheer pleasure of it, and for the cleansing and renewal the water offers, some of us walk the seashore. Others, such as Thoreau, find peace and perspective at their own Walden Pond. And there are those of us who go to the rivers that are home. Few writers have conveyed their experience better than Nick Lyons, author of *Bright Rivers*, teacher by day, writer at night, "a juggler, flinging my separate lives high and careless into the air." Daydreaming at work, he says:

I catch a glimpse of them, inside. Deep within me they uncoil. . . . Rivers. . . . Bright green live rivers. . . .

Nothing in this world so enlivens my spirit and emotions as the rivers I know. They are necessities. In their clear, swift or slow, generous or coy waters, I regain my powers. I find again those parts of myself that have been lost in cities. Stillness. Patience. Green thoughts. Open eyes. Attachment. High drama. Earthiness. Wit. The Huck Finn I once was. Gentleness. "The life of things." . . . Amen.

We must stay in touch with the living waters to keep our souls fresh and moist.

2

WHERE AM I IN MY LIFE?

*You walker, there are no roads, only wind
trails on the sea.*
                                    —ANTONIO MACHADO
                                    translation by Robert Bly

*When we become enlightened, we do not become
perfect and live in Paradise. Enlightenment
offers the possibility of living with the acceptance of imperfection. There is only this life and
some happiness is possible.*
                                    —SHELDON KOPP

April 1

THE YOUNG entertainer John Belushi seemed to have everything to live for. But on the night he died, if the stories are true, Belushi asked his driver to take him around town, saying, "Find me someone who needs me." Later that night, he died of a drug overdose.

Belushi might just as well have been asking, "Find me someone who will give my life meaning." From outward appearances, he was the kind of person Rabbi Kushner was writing to in his book, *When All You've Ever Wanted Isn't Enough*. The book is subtitled, *The Search for a Life That Matters*.

Unfortunately, many people spend a good portion of their time waiting for someone to give their lives meaning. And sadly, maybe they could find their own answer if they rephrased the question: "Who is supposed to find meaning for my life?"

The meaning of life comes from how we live it.

A LIFE of your own does not mean having your way all the time, especially when you live with people you love. There is give and take that goes with loving others. The alternation of giving and receiving care is not the same thing as giving up or giving in. You are still responsible for your feelings, for your actions. And in the context of marriage and family you may assume responsibility to provide for and/or care for others. But what kind? How much? For how long?

In *The Road Less Traveled*, Dr. Scott Peck comments, "Distinguishing what we are and what we are not responsible for in this life is one of the greatest problems of human existence. It is never completely solved; for the entirety of our lives we must continually assess and reassess where our responsibilities lie in the ever-changing course of events."

What we get out of life depends on what we are willing to give to it.

April 3

SPIRITUAL PILGRIMS, past and present, are as human as the rest of us. We must learn from their humanity as well as from their holiness. They too can fail or become corrupt. Like them, we will be unable to transcend the human limits of momentary spiritual grace; yet, if we accept the inevitability of our fall, we may rise again.

During troubled times in our spiritual lives, often the wisest, strongest thing we can do is ask for a hand to help us get back on our feet again. In turn, we can assist others when they fall. Truly helping people begins by simply being willing to be with them, to get to know them as individuals, to let them know us. We must live our truth, rather than try to persuade them of our beliefs. And, without retreating, we must be willing to face the possibility of being personally vulnerable to them simply as other human beings by taking the risk of their becoming truly important in our lives.

We don't have to be weak to seek help or strong to offer it.

IN HIS short story, "The Country of the Blind," H. G. Wells illustrates the power and menace of collective thinking. In a mysterious mountain valley, everyone was born blind. Their waking period was night; they slept during the day. All their ways of living were contrived to meet their needs.

Nunez, a mountain climber, was their first visitor when he accidentally fell into the valley. Able to see, he thought he'd have a great advantage over the valley dwellers, but instead they thought he was the one who was handicapped. They moved through the darkness with grace and confidence, while he could only stumble along uncertainly.

As time passed, Nunez grew lonely and insecure, longing to be accepted. Eventually, he fell in love, wanted to marry, and stay. The village elders finally agreed, but to cure his "peculiarities," they offered to remove his eyes. Nunez was horrified. It was so hard to go on trusting himself and to keep clear in his mind that he made mistakes only because he could see. It took all his strength to turn away and make the lonely, dangerous climb out of their happy valley.

Being ourselves while still accepting others is one of the hardest things we can do.

April 5

IF ONLY I tried harder, worked harder, really cared, truly wanted to, couldn't I become that wonderful person whose worth would be validated by others who know me? They would approve of me and love me, and then finally I could feel good about myself, too. Right?

But what if, instead, I didn't wait around for a unanimous vote of approval from *them*? If I accept myself as an ordinary human being, a pretty decent, usually competent person who, like everyone else, can feel overwhelmed, make mistakes, and sometimes play the fool, then I am free from the needless shame and guilt at not having attained an unachievable goal. I am also free to do what I want, rather than what I think I should, or what I think others expect of me. I will undoubtedly be exposed for who I really am, but would that be so awful?

Inner power has far less to do with pleasing others than doing as you please.

WHEN YOU feel safe enough to face the hidden aspects of who you are, you are much more able to accept yourself. Then, your personal freedom expands, and you suffer far less from defensive denial.

No one accepts his or her self completely. We are burdened by opposing forces within our contradictory natures. This is further complicated by the needs of those we love versus our own needs.

The problem with not being honest with yourself about who you are is, among others, that your life becomes a series of frenzied alterations between sacrificially working at work and superficially playing at play.

All of us are vulnerable in our own ways.

April 7

IT'S HARD to know how to help people. Often our reasons for wanting to help have more to do with making us feel good about ourselves than with our concern for their well-being. Some of us fulfill our own needs for self-esteem by trying unnecessarily elaborate heroic rescue missions when giving a hand quietly and simply would do. Another ulterior motive we might have for helping is trying to control the situation or the other person.

When we imagine that we know what's best for other people, even our best intended efforts can be damaging. But, if we simply help them see options that have been overlooked and then support whatever choice they make, our assistance is offered with genuine respect.

Sometimes, we have nothing more to offer than to acknowledge our own helplessness to solve their problems and stand by them anyway. Being willing to be there with them may be all the help we have to offer. When hurting people discover there is even one person who cares enough to be open to their agony, it comforts them and encourages them to endure.

Revealing our own helplessness may be all the help we have to offer and it may be all the help the other person needs.

IN ANCIENT China, philosophers and sages of many different schools were concerned with a single central question: "How are we to live in a chaotic world, dominated by human suffering?" The answer offered by the Taoist masters was: "Free yourself from the world."

This freeing did not imply denial of reality or flight from it. Rather freedom lay in achieving a state of mind where a person no longer struggled, and so merged with the Tao, the Way of Life underlying man, Nature, and the Universe. The masters didn't explain how to accomplish this, but told parables or stories instead. For example: There once was a one-legged dragon named Kui, whose envy of a centipede led him to ask, "How can you possibly manage a hundred legs, when I manage my one leg with difficulty?" "It is so simple," replied the centipede. "I do not manage them at all. They land all over the place like drops of spit."

To learn to live skillfully, with grace, we must stop thinking about what we're supposed to do at each point and do what comes naturally instead.

When we're self-conscious, we get in our own way.

April 9

LIVING IN the shadow of shame is a miserable existence, but it is not an irreversible way of life. To make a major shift from feeling predominantly shameful to primarily self-accepting, we must find ways to bring light to dark places. Ironically, it is only by looking into the shadows of our selves and reclaiming all we have disowned that we can heal ugly wounds. The deepest, most lasting of this work requires a return to the borderland.

The psychological borderland is a transitional zone, a lawless frontier beyond the conventional authority of reason and morality. Here, nothing is unthinkable; right and wrong are ignored. Metaphorically, it is a seedy carnival, where clowns and con artists emerge in antic anarchy. As adults, we must step forward to meet the bad, awkward, or embarrassing strangers in the twilight and welcome with acceptance, not shame, those seedy characters who are also us.

Acknowledging our weaknesses makes us stronger. If our wounds are to heal, it is not our bandages but our open, running sores that must be exposed to air and light.

Make a friend of the enemy within.

WE ALL suffer some unavoidable losses. People we love die, close friends move away, and, despite our best efforts, some of the ventures we undertake don't work out. What's a person to do when he or she suffers a bad break?

We can complain, but fussing doesn't change anything. If we accept our losses, we grieve by crying about them. Crying doesn't help either. That's why we cry—because nothing helps.

But grieving does allow us to bury our dead and to get beyond our disappointments. This leaves room in our hearts that we may be able to fill with love for someone else or hope for some new undertaking, but we cannot hurry our pain or rush our willingness to begin anew.

We need to move on in our lives in search of whatever is available that makes us happy, but a major loss leaves a hole in our heart—a hole that can never be completely refilled.

We cannot simply substitute one hope or one love for another.

IN AN old Chinese tale, a woodcutter kills a deer in the forest. He hides the carcass until his wood is cut, but when he can't find it later, he decides he must have dreamed about the deer. Walking home, he mutters aloud about the appearance and disappearance of good fortune.

A passing farmer overhears him, searches, and finds the deer. At home, the farmer tells his wife about the woodcutter who thought he had only dreamed he'd killed a deer. His wife says, "Why dream there was a woodcutter? You have the deer." That night the woodcutter dreams about his lost deer and the farmer who found it. The following morning, he confronts the farmer, but to no avail, and so they end up in court.

The chief justice listens to their story: The woodcutter kills a deer, dreams he didn't, then dreams he did; the farmer has a deer, but his wife says he is dreaming that someone else might have caught it. In his wisdom, the justice admits he cannot tell who is and isn't dreaming. All he knows for sure is "here we have the deer" and so decides that they should split it.

Who knows who's right and who's wrong?

No one is free of fear. When we enter unfamiliar situations, undertake changes in our attitudes or actions, or open ourselves to greater intimacy with another person, we may feel excited, but we also feel anxious.

Hemingway's definition of courage as "grace under pressure," does not imply the absence of fear. It is only when we do what feels right even though we are afraid that we are entitled to see ourselves as courageous.

There is no shame in accepting that some particular undertaking scares you too much to try it. But when you face your fear openly, you may find it sufficiently diminished to allow you to see some otherwise obscured aspect of yourself that then takes priority. For example, when you face your fear that letting someone know you better might result in rejection, the loneliness of your isolation can give you the courage to show more of yourself.

Taking risks by denying our fears is reckless. Taking risks by facing our fears is courageous.

April 13

DURING THE early years of his final incarnation, the young Buddha's family protected him from ever encountering illness, aging, or death, and so he didn't know what fear was. After a long while, he saw an old man, a sick man, and a corpse. Instead of running away in fear, he decided to spend his life searching for some way to free people from being trapped on the wheel of life's sorrows.

After years of trying, the Buddha seated himself under the Tree of Enlightenment. It was there that the Evil One tried to tempt him, first with lust, greed, ambition, and then with fame. Next came an assault by terrible armies of dark and devouring monsters. Unmoved, the Buddha remained safe by raising his right hand against fear.

At last, the god of death and desire offered another temptation: protection from pain and suffering. But Buddha extended his other hand in compassion and announced his final decision: He would go on facing his fears in this life, so that the protection of his understanding would remain available until the last of us had also attained enlightenment.

When it comes to fear, the way out is in.

WHEN WE believe we are right, we feel competent, at times powerful. But never believing that we are wrong is another issue altogether. Never being wrong means either you already have all the answers or you can never make a mistake. Having the strength of one's convictions is different from an attitude of unquestioning, absolute certainty.

Have you ever wondered why you started feeling that you needed to be right? Was it a need to be strong enough to protect yourself against all odds? The need to have strength for survival may well have been real—it may still be very real—but ironically so much of that useful strength is needlessly sapped when you have to remain on guard, cautious about being ambushed by someone or something who knows something you don't.

What would happen to your position of power if you admitted uncertainty or if you used defensive energy to take the offense instead? The worst that might happen is you might learn that there is more to learn. The best outcome would be that you'd learn you weren't dangerously vulnerable by being open to learning.

We cannot know what we do not know.

April 15

LIFE CAN be counted on to provide all the pain that anyone might possibly need. Even so, people invariably add needless suffering to their already heavy burden.

Some are in the habit of anguishing over what might have been. Some lie awake nights, worrying in advance about catastrophies that may come. Others complain that they don't deserve whatever problems they have, adding a sense of personal injustice to their pain.

Longing for the good old days when we feel certain life was better, and petulantly hoping for a future when everything will be right again, we ignore opportunities for joy offered by the present. We compound our misery with the feeling that life is passing us by and then we wonder why.

Yet, unless we pay attention to what we're doing right now, we're choosing by default to miss out on our chance to make what we can of whatever we have.

Longing for the past, dreaming about the future, we pass up the present.

WE GO through the adolescent crisis of discovering that life is not what we thought it was. Suddenly nothing makes sense anymore, and we stand nakedly vulnerable to the rawness of a life without meaning.

Transitional periods are difficult at any age. The insect's molting offers a good metaphor for the human's periodic shedding of protective layers of innocence. Without these losses, there would be no possibility of increased awareness and expanded freedom. Yet each loss is accompanied by a period of vulnerability. Some forms of madness are no more than failed transitions from one vision of life to the next.

Opportunities for further growth present themselves again and again. If we aren't ready to accept the helplessness required for a particular transformation, then that opportunity must be set aside for a time. The necessary delays in our awakening are natural phases we pass through, unless we get stuck somehow and one phase lasts a lifetime.

Everything is difficult at first.

April 17

LIFE IS so complicated. There doesn't seem to be any way for any of us to get through a day without spending some part of it playing out temporary parts. We perform rehearsed social roles or even personal interactions that don't engage or reveal very much of who we really are. Sometimes we confuse the actor with the part, or the self with the mask. Then we risk losing our way in a house of mirrors where we mistake illusion for reality.

For some of us, the taking on of roles evolves into a chronic, lifetime acting out of a neurotic personal "tragedy," suffering as serious-minded, supervirtuous heroes. Only when we discover the absurdity of our needless, neurotic suffering can we save ourselves from a lifelong role, playing at being the tragic hero. Comedy, not tragedy, is the crucial emotional release.

Life is too important to be taken too seriously.

WHAT IS crazy and what isn't? These standards were painfully established and aren't easily suspended. As children, we learned that when our behavior made our parents mildly uncomfortable, whatever we did was discounted as "silly" and made us feel foolish. But, when we did things that upset our parents deeply, they called us "crazy," a characterization that threatened to discredit our whole beings. Few children can handle the risk of a shattered self-image, so we did our best to avoid risking disapproval. If we stopped acting crazy then, now we are likely to deny how irrational we can sometimes be. Instead, we reassure ourselves by judging others as strange.

Many people found solace with one friend or a group of friends who supported a mutual definition of themselves as sane and all others as crazy. They bonded together, isolating themselves from other groups.

Now, we may be able to escape suffering these extremes. Still, we all will be faced with internal contradictions between self-expression and conventional behavior, between reason and imagination, and our wishes to merge while yet retaining our separate identities.

Worrying too much about seeming weird can drive you crazy.

April 19

LIFE WITHOUT play would be unbearably dreary. Being serious, realistic, and grown-up (whatever that may mean) have their place and their own rewards. But, in the absence of play, all of this will not only make Jack and Jill dull boys and girls but may make them stuffy, pompous adults as well.

When play involves two or more people, a mutual understanding is needed that "This is play!" If one person misunderstands the other, both may find themselves in trouble—needless fights, awkward situations, embarrassment, and hurt feelings.

When two people play together, it can be great fun, or it can be highly destructive. It is safe and rewarding to play games if we both know that we are only playing, if neither of us is forced to play against our will, and if neither insists on changing the rules without mutual consent.

Games can be good for us as long as everyone involved knows we're playing.

THE INITIAL love of a parent is accepted by a child in all innocence as a state of grace. But when, for whatever reasons, we fall from grace, we have to live in a world in which the experience of feeling really loved is lost. In the face of the questions, "Was I really loved? Was I fooled? Did I fool myself?" there follows a life of searching for someone who really cares.

Unfortunately, until we resolve our fear of betrayal born of the first abandonment, bolstered by the feeling that we were to blame, we perennially distrust whatever love is given. The final irony is that when we find someone to love, the person we choose usually contributes to the problem, not the solution. We are more likely to feel really loved by someone who is erratic in how they treat us. Being treated well in a continuing way is something we find hard to bear because it echoes the grief of love once had and now lost.

Even in love, be careful what you wish for or you might get it.

April 21

IN LIFE, as in theater, actors' identities are transformed by the roles they play. When we are very young, we are most vulnerable to being assigned parts we would not otherwise choose. However, we may lose our identity even when we're grown, if we are immersed in a setting so compelling that our usual ways of being fall away. So, for example, in a life-threatening crisis, a lifelong coward may become a leader and a rescuer, whereas one who is usually strong may be transformed into a helpless victim.

In these extreme situations, life seems so painfully ambiguous we grasp at any context that will offer the illusion of identity, certainty, and stability. In order not to make a serious error in judgment or do something that will cause us more pain in the end, the best course is to acknowledge our state of confusion and admit to ourselves that we feel overwhelmed. In time, there may be some kind of value from this experience, but for the moment, we can learn what it means to take care of ourselves—to do the minimum needed for survival, be patient with ourselves, and try not to add further injury.

Sometimes doing nothing is better than doing something foolish.

EVEN WITH our closest, most trusted personal relationships, we are rarely completely open, showing our true reflection, without trying to hide the blemishes that we feel certain detract from our attractiveness. This mask is more revealing than those we wear with casual acquaintances, so we hide only those excesses and deficiencies that we believe will be unacceptable to our loved ones or ourselves. Each of us is aware of things about ourselves that seem too awful to acknowledge to anyone else. Some of these thoughts and feelings are never openly expressed. Secrets such as these are examined only in the safety of solitude, if we are willing to admit them even to ourselves.

There are some losses even more damaging than missing out on other people's acceptance of who we are. The missed opportunities we risk when we deceive others are slight compared with the needless suffering that comes from fooling ourselves.

None of us feels safe being completely open.

April 23

DEFINING WHO you are began before you were born. From the moment of conception you were graced with your biologically predetermined characteristics, ranging from eye color to temperament.

To these inborn parameters were added your waiting family's fantasy projections. Very soon after your birth, the myths that were to shape your life were announced and confirmed. ("See, he has grandpa's smile"; "She's such a good-natured baby"; "He's only happy when I'm holding him"; "She's never satisfied.") Burdened or supported by your family's projections of aspects of themselves, whatever you did was taken to be further confirmation of your already assigned identity.

At very early, tender ages, you were exquisitely vulnerable to being shaped by those around you, including their beliefs about who it was all right for you to be. Before you knew who you were or even *that* you were, you were already learning who you were supposed to be.

We must be careful not to allow others to decide who we are to be. How can you be sure you are who you think you are?

UNLESS WE become aware of ourselves and accept our unconscious shadow sides, we are certain to find ourselves at the mercy of their powerful, primitive demands.

Remaining unconscious of these disowned parts of ourselves is both costly and dangerous. No matter how hard we try, we can never fully eliminate the chance that these forbidden impulses will break out now and then. In other words, demands that are not faced within ourselves will be confronted unexpectedly in the world about us.

We have animal instincts and impulses. To get some measure of personal power and freedom, we must begin the difficult work of accepting that fact. The *I Ching* says:

> *Contemplation of my life*
> *Decides the choice*
> *Between advance and retreat.*
> *Hidden dragon. Do not act.*

No matter how well we cover up, at times our inadequacies will be exposed.

April 25

HIDDEN SAFELY in your personal shadow are all of the ideas, feelings, and wishes that, if expressed, could have placed you in jeopardy in your early childhood. You had no choice but to disown those parts of yourself that might have offended those who took care of you. It was unsafe even to be aware of the existence of these risky notions.

The more one of your parents was threatened by anything about you, the more completely it had to be repressed. So, gradually your personal shadow became a repository for what you were led to believe to be the negative side of your personality. In reality, it is merely the rest of you. Together, you and your shadow make a complete self.

Your shadow may contain lost vitality and highly personal creative possibilities. It also holds the answers to everything you always wanted to know about yourself but were afraid to ask.

It's not easy to admit we're capable of doing what we want to believe we aren't.

WHEN WE see life as divided into endlessly opposing forces of light and dark, good and evil, life and death, these polarities seem to be intrinsically fated to remain continuously in conflict.

These struggles are experienced as going on within us as well as in the world around us. Some aspects of the inner struggles we own as self; others we disclaim as not-self.

People have always been faced with resolving critical problems of self-acceptance. When we acknowledge all the opposing forces that exist within us, these turn out to be as hard to reconcile as their counterparts in the world around us. Even when the good guys appear to be winning for a while, too soon the tide of battle shifts. Isn't there any lasting peace?

There is no life without struggle, but one seeker can help another and together they can make a journey neither could make alone.

April 27

ORDINARILY, THINKING about feeling is enough to dampen passion. Even when things are going well, obsessional characters tend to think elaborately, rather than to feel. Under pressure, we may escalate into the rather desperate refinement of thinking only about thinking. Even that more elegant defensive maneuver may prove insufficient for totally suppressing the tumultuous emotional life that we are attempting to disown.

Desperate times call for desperate measures. If our efforts to avoid uncontrolled feelings have failed, more of our energy may be drained away into a morass of debilitating depression. We may dream up irrational fears as a security measure to avoid risky, impulsive actions. Or we may immerse ourselves in isolating addictions that quiet our secret longing without acknowledging the emotional hunger they represent. In any event, it's possible to maintain a self divided by conscious thought and ignored emotion, but the cost is exorbitant.

What if God doesn't want us to be caged in our lusts but to be free in them?

How much of our lives do we spend trying to avoid the risk of being embarrassed? No matter how well we dramatize our toughness or restrict our lives, secretly we remain as vulnerable as ever to the possibility of being exposed as a person who makes mistakes.

There is really no escape. One of the things we can count on in this life is that we will make mistakes and feel foolish at times. We may feel such discomfort and we wish we would die, but we won't.

The distress of embarrassment is felt when we're unable to cope with some situation in the presence of others. But, the standard for how well we should be able to cope is our own—what we expect of ourselves, as well as what we believe our audience expects of us.

To resolve our predicament, we can think of ourselves as completely inadequate, always doing something stupid. Or we can stay rigidly restricted, hiding our errors as best as we can. A third choice is to accept the inevitable—that we are ordinary human beings who will fumble from time to time—and find better things to worry about.

Be confident that you will continue to make mistakes and learn to live with your frailties.

April 29

MANY PEOPLE complain that what they fear most is rejection. Often they are astonished to discover that their true, underlying problem is just the opposite. What is most frightening is not rejection but acceptance, not failure but success.

If you begin to pursue what you want in life, and you find your efforts rewarded by being accepted and treated well by other people, you feel uncomfortable. Somehow you've learned to discredit pleasurable experiences, believing you don't deserve them. It's as though you're not entitled to what you want most.

Believing that you are not worthy of feeling good, you're stuck in a vicious cycle kept in motion by your self-defeating attitude. When you're feeling pain, you seek relief, but any comfort you receive seems so unwarranted that it just makes you uncomfortable all over again. If you are to escape this kind of double bind, you'll have to reconsider your beliefs about yourself. What if you simply haven't recognized that you're really a good, valuable human being?

Not feeling good about yourself doesn't necessarily prove you're a bad person.

PLATO'S TALE of Androgyne is a light-hearted mythic account of the origins of the incompleteness we experience in the absence of the other. Zeus originally cut man in two, the story goes, to diminish his strength and humble his pride. But once apart, one half couldn't survive without the other. So Apollo was ordered to make one of the halves into a woman.

Plato's original intent was to focus on how we pursue a beloved as if he or she made up the missing half of our divided self. The problem is that's what some of us do.

The joys of loving others are real and wonderful, but too often we miss out on opportunities for love because we actually believe we need that other person to make up for our inadequacies and to give us self-worth. If we feel compelled to find this person, our drive may repel someone we might otherwise attract.

When we find someone who loves us in return, then relying on the person to fill us or fix us makes our relationship more desperate than it needs to be and jeopardizes what might have been a beautiful romance.

Before we are able to love freely, we must feel sufficient to ourselves.

May 1

WHENEVER WE are having fun, time flies. When we are troubled, time drags on so slowly that the discomfort seems as if it will never end. Any attempt to alter our sense of the ebb and flow of time automatically exaggerates its pace. If we try to make the good moments last, they disappear like the wail of a passing train. Attempts to speed the passage of the bad moments only serves to slow them down even more.

In spite of everything we try, life remains unpredictably uneven, with periods of easy living disrupted by troubled times. Unexpected changes catch us unprepared. Each moment requires its own solution.

If we want to spare ourselves the suffering of unmet expectations, we must never forget that there is no life without problems, no joy without sorrow. Remembering this allows us to feel less arrogant when things are going well and less inadequate when we run into unexpected trouble.

Feeling fully alive doesn't depend on what we believe in but on how we experience each great and small moment in our lives.

ONCE SEVERAL members of a Hasidic congregation had become helplessly lost in a dense forest. They were delighted when unexpectedly they came upon their rabbi who was also wandering through the woods. They implored, "Master, we are lost! Please show us the way out of the forest."

The rabbi replied, "I do not know the way out either, but I do know which paths lead nowhere. I will show you the ways that won't work, and then perhaps together we can discover the ones that do."

Another spiritual leader, Teilhard de Chardin, wrote, "We are one, after all, you and I; together we suffer, together exist, and forever will re-create each other."

We have only ourselves and one another. That may not be much, but that's all there is.

May 3

CHANGE IS usually upsetting or at least stressful, even if the change is for the better. But, beware of asking that things remain the same lest the fates fulfill that invitation to boredom.

Once we get used to change, we are better able to realize the richness, color, depth, and intensity of life's experiences instead of being undone or upset by the lack of continuity. Even the return of things as we knew them requires us to tolerate change.

But if we aren't prepared for the haphazard events that turn us this way and that, upside down and inside out, we tend to regard them as "moments in my life," as opposed to "interruptions of my life." A similar point was made by Adela Rogers St. Johns, the late journalist and author: "We have to learn to be happy in spite of things, not because of things."

The search for happiness isn't a simple, uninterrupted upward ascent.

WHEN YOU'RE feeling bad, let it show. Help may come from unexpected sources. Of course, there will be people who don't want to deal with your pain or the pain within themselves. They will tell you to cheer up because things will be better after a while. That doesn't help much when you're depressed.

But, there will be others who understand what it's like to have the blues. They will acknowledge how hopeless you must feel and share experiences of times that they too felt down and out. Because they don't try to change how you feel, having people like that around can help a lot.

Another unexpected helper comes from deep down inside us. Our inner voice acknowledges our troubling experiences. We have escaped from them for so long that when they overtook us it was like getting caught in a flood. But like flood waters do, the depressed feelings will subside.

We have our own answers, but sometimes they lie buried deep inside.

May 5

IN "The Mysterious Stranger," a short story by Mark Twain, two young boys are playing on a riverbank outside of town when Satan appears as a stranger/angel, and offers to grant them a wish. Downstream they see an old man, who has suffered long and hard, as everyone in the village knows. So, the boys point to him and tell the stranger their wish—to make the man completely happy.

Sometime later, the boys learn that the old man has completely lost his senses—he's now a lunatic, a smiling "idiot." Back on the riverbank, the stranger appears and the boys confront him angrily. "But," responds the devilish angel, "I did grant your wish. How else could anyone be totally happy in this life?"

There is no uninterrupted happiness; there is no perfect peace. Ironically, whatever peace there might be comes from accepting the good and bad nature of who we are, as well as the lucky and unlucky quality of our lives.

Having problems is part of living.

TIME AND time again we get our hopes up only to be disappointed once more. Why do we do this to ourselves? Will we never learn? Dr. Maurice Friedman, in his book *A Dialogue with Hasidic Tales*, wrote that "Expectation and disappointment point . . . to understanding hope and despondency as the tension between the present and the future."

"But it may be," Dr. Friedman continued, "that real hope is not tied to the future at all, that it resides . . . in the present." Living in the present is the only antidote to the unsound expectation that ties us forever to the future and makes it inevitable, as Pascal said, that we should be forever unhappy.

Courage and trust soothe the creative tension between present and future, expectation and disappointment, living and dying, meaning and absurdity.

Expecting more than we can get invites disappointment.

"IF ONLY I was wise enough, I'd make no mistakes. If somehow I was good enough, I would be safe from misfortune. If someone else would only take good enough care of me, then I could be protected from upsetting experiences." Self-pity is a hazard of hypothetical longings.

Wishing for a life uninterrupted by random mishaps and personal hang-ups only makes matters worse, just as turning our backs to the oncoming surf assures us we'll get washed over and probably knocked off our feet again. The illusion that if we try harder or worry more we'll eventually get control is deceptive and ineffective.

Ignoring the tides of trouble and disorder that will come, we miss out on the opportunities offered by facing those experiences, just as facing the waves and becoming a skilled swimmer leaves us feeling strong and competent. Knowing both our strengths and the limits of our abilities, we learn how best to cope with most of the challenges our lives will offer.

Longing for a life without sorrow merely makes present matters worse.

WHEN SOMEONE hurts us, we want to hurt them back. It may be an understandable reaction, but sometimes it does more harm to the avenger than it does to the one we set out to punish. A clear example is that of people who feel that their parents neglected or abused them when they were young.

Some grow up to be adults who continue feeling unworthy or deprived. Because they remain committed to getting back at their parents, they stubbornly refuse to take better care of themselves. They act as if attaining self-esteem and happiness on their own would let their parents off the hook. If they should succeed as grown-ups, then their parents could say, "See, we didn't do such a bad job of raising you after all!"

Rather than allow our parents to get away with feeling good, some of us spitefully settle for feeling bad about ourselves. Doing this, we've made the choice to continue our own needless suffering.

Living well is the best revenge.

May 9

LAUGHING AT our past foolishness allows us to realize truths too simple, obvious, and natural to be grasped when we are taking ourselves too seriously. Self-importance is a trap from which we can only be sprung by the antic irreverence of laughter.

Each mishap is an opportunity to learn if we are open to reconsidering the source of our discomfort. A Sufi tale illustrates how it can happen that out of each unfortunate situation comes its own remedy: A monkey threw a coconut from a treetop at a hungry Sufi, and it hit him on his leg. The man picked it up, drank the milk, ate the meat, and made a bowl from the shell.

Nothing can be had without paying for it. When any of us makes a mistake, we have simply paid in advance for that which we may yet acquire. To gain from misfortune caused by our foolishness we need a sense of humor that affords a clearer perspective of what good can come of it, and the willingness to look at ourselves in a new light.

Every loss plants a seed for new growth.

WHEN PEOPLE give the appearance of having saintly virtue and heroic intentions, we have to wonder what else they are. No human being is completely pure in thought, word, or action. People who want us to think they are angels aren't to be trusted.

Whatever conscious attitudes individuals have, the exact opposites exist in their unconscious. The more extreme and seemingly pure the conscious appears, the more energy it takes to contain its exactly equivalent counterpart. And, the greater danger that some time, unexpectedly, the denied impulses may break loose in full savagery.

Being on our own, we must take personal responsibility for coming to know the wolf within us. Otherwise, we are tempted to put on sheep's clothing and slaughter, or at least have a damaging effect on the lives of the rest of the flock.

Better to be too true to be good than too good to be true.

May 11

A PERSON can be a long way past childhood and still be intimidated by an overwhelming sense of powerlessness when faced with a head-on view of his or her place in the universe. The full force of our individual insignificance is almost too much to bear.

Protecting ourselves with simplistic beliefs keeps us from feeling helplessly vulnerable. Then, if we stubbornly ignore or deny the disappointment of our lives as they are, we can go on believing that life is the fairy tale we want it to be. In our storybook world, virtue will be rewarded and evil punished. We can make someone take care of us. All we have to do is be good enough.

But if we want to grow up and increase our freedom to find what happiness we might in this world as it is, each of us must give up believing in fairy tales and go through repeated losses of innocence.

When we wait for a happy ending, we only waste our lives.

FEELING ALONE, helpless, and afraid is merely the ordinary state of affairs. Remembering that everyone else is in the same situation helps a little—but not a whole lot.

No creatures are able to control their own lives, but of all life forms, only humans are aware of their predicament. We know that too soon we will die, and that after a short while no one will even remember our having lived.

While some animals appear able to enjoy being warm and fed, only humans are capable of worrying about whether or not the moment will last, wondering what it is really all about, or becoming distracted by comparing that moment with some other.

Clearly, imagination is both a crown and a cross. Seeing what is possible allows us to improve our lot. But unless we're very careful, in the process of trying to get better, we give up accepting any good moment with grace.

We must learn to live each moment as it comes.

May 13

PEOPLE HAVE always had the need to share their secrets with others, especially those secrets they feel guilty about. In sharing, we seek relief from our loneliness, reassurance about our worth, and release from our guilt. In the very early Christian church, personal confession was made in public. People lived close together in small communities and often their sins were against their neighbors. When offenders confessed in front of the ones they offended, most often the community was reconciled, wrongs were redressed, and the ill feelings of both parties could be resolved.

An Alcoholics Anonymous slogan says, "We are as sick as our secrets." The Twelve Steps offer a specific process for identifying secrets, admitting them, and making amends. Of course, alcoholics aren't the only ones with wrongdoings to hide. All of us have done things we think must be kept secret. We guard our secrets while blackmailing ourselves with guilt. This drains our energy, restricts our freedom, and has no useful purpose except, perhaps, what we gain from experiencing the process of seeking relief.

There is personal power in being transparent.

THE RENAISSANCE was a time of freedom that came as a trade-off for the certainty of the absolute values of the Middle Ages. Montaigne offered help for the Renaissance man to come to know and evaluate his personal self by putting no one else's authority above the teachings of his own experience. "The life of Caesar has no more of a lesson for us than our own; and whether an emperor's or an ordinary man's, it is still a life that is subject to all accidents. Let us just listen to it: We tell ourselves all that we chiefly need." To deflate idealism even more, he added, "Kings and philosophers defecate, and ladies too."

Montaigne stressed that in the midst of the most active life, people must have private thoughts, a necessity for independent judgment. A part of everyone must be free of other's eyes. A part of our self must be all our own. The idea was not a suggestion to withhold from others but to joyfully celebrate our own special self. Montaigne said, "We seek other conditions because we do not understand the use of our own, and go out of ourselves because we do not know what it is like within."

We already have all that we need.

AN UNHAPPY childhood is not a justification for an unlived adult life. At best, life is a mixed bag for everyone. All of us face disappointment, frustration, failure, betrayal, illness, aging, and finally our own death. Yet, we must face up to the challenge from Camus: "to be a just man in an unjust world."

Life is arbitrary and we have to take things as they are, bring to them what we can, and enjoy them as they stand. This is it, often unsatisfying, always imperfect. But it's the only world we have.

Can you be loving in this world and bring to it the meaning of your own being and willingness? Can you live and love without illusions in a world where there is no appeal? Can you love in the absence of illusions?

To take the challenge, simple insights—deceptive because they are too fundamental to be grasped entirely—must be learned, not just once but again and again. As Hemingway said, "There are some things which cannot be learned quickly, and time, which is all we have, must be paid heavily for their acquiring."

While you're wondering how well you're doing, you miss the opportunity to experience what you're doing.

EVERY DAY we are confronted with alternatives to accept or reject. These range from trivial options such as what we'll have for dessert or which jacket we'll wear to crucial career changes and commitments to personal relationships.

The lesser choices can only add to or limit our small pleasures. If we struggle over each selection, we end up squandering our energy by obsessing away our lives.

The greater issues may have long-term consequences that influence the quality of our futures. These decisions are best made after a thoughtful inventory of who we are and who we want to become.

A choice of dessert is a matter of a moment's whim that can be safely made without knowing much about what we're picking. Deciding which path our lives are to take requires that we examine our motives carefully, in light of a deep understanding of ourselves.

Before we can be free, we must accept responsibility for the choices we make.

May 17

As IF it weren't enough to struggle through the confusion of childhood, once we emerge, we realize truth remains elusive. For one thing, we all are vulnerable. Each is as weak and as strong as the other, as tough and as tender, as capable of good and of evil. We are all fully responsible for whatever we do.

Ultimately, we are alone. No one can do for us what we must do for ourselves. No one else's solution will do. We all have to contend with the same fundamental condition of being here, and now, and our self and no other. For each of us it is different, and for each it is also the same. Individual lives differ mainly in that I am not you and you are not me, yet together we both have to go it alone.

> *You got to walk that lonesome valley,*
> *You got to walk it by yourself;*
> *Nobody else can walk it for you,*
> *You got to walk it by yourself.*

We're all in this alone.

THERE IS no way to get past hazardous temptations once and for all, particularly the tendency to depend on others for our welfare. The wish to be taken care of never dies, nor does the wish to find the flawless leader, who will function as a perfect parent so we can imagine that our worries are over for good.

Irreverence—the freedom from taking anything or anyone too seriously—is the best protection against falling into an authority trap of our own making. There are no truths that can't be questioned, no law or custom that can't be debated, nothing so sacred that we can't see the humor in it. A playful attitude will help break through pretense without hurting another person any more than is absolutely required by the question we need to ask.

As we ad lib our way through a world in flux, again and again having to reconcile the polarities of responsibility and freedom, playful irreverence helps us learn not to take ourselves too seriously.

Laughter is the sound of freedom.

FEELING PROUD or ashamed of another person means that his or her separation from your self is incomplete. The relationship is less like love than emotional exploitation.

Relationships between adults that are not exploitive depend on well-defined boundaries between one self and another. When it is clear that I am I and you are you, I have no need to try to manipulate our images in each other's eyes. If I understand that feeling good doesn't depend on your reaction to me, but on what I think of myself, I retain the power over my own self-image. The more clearly I remain in charge of myself, the more you can trust that what I offer you is freely given.

My ability to give will be proportionate to my freedom to withhold. If I try to please you as a way to get what I need, it won't help me and it will cost you something. Whatever I give you freely is yours to keep.

If we are ever to be truly together, first we have to be clearly separate selves.

GROPING OUR way through life, we may be no better off than the proverbial group of blind men who try to agree on the definition of an elephant while each touches a different part. Blind ourselves in many ways, we cannot even be sure that there is an elephant.

How then are we to cope with these differences between imagination and reality? To begin with, we can recognize that what we imagine is not necessarily unreal. If we feel the trunk of the elephant and describe it as an animal with a long flexible appendage, we aren't wrong.

When we realize that our reality is just one way of seeing things, and that it is no more good or true than anyone else's, it helps us to cope with life's ambiguities. If we don't have to try to make one rigid vision of life fit all kinds of situations, and we get past insisting that our view is the only true reality, we can then respect and learn from the experience of others.

Beware of those times when your way of seeing things seems like the only truth.

May 21

EASY TIMES are sweet. Hard times are bitter. Bittersweet mixtures occur every so often for everyone. As times change, we are faced with choices, first to deal with the transition and then with the new situation. The many gods of Hinduism offer an array of alternatives. We don't have to believe in the existence of these gods to benefit from what their metaphors can teach us.

As the origin of everything that is, Brahma reminds us that all is one. In his form as the sweet spirit of eternal youth, Krishna invites the acceptance of joy as natural. In the form of Kali, the goddess of troubled times, we are shown that it is necessary for us to slow down enough to examine what is wrong. Demonstrating how annihilation of old attitudes allows new ways, she opens us to opportunities offered by disruption.

Remembering these changing gods has practical value for us when we have to make a major personal change. It helps if we recognize the nature of our changing situations and then, like the gods, adopt an attitude that allows us to profit from living each present moment as it comes.

We must learn to enjoy the sweet moments in our lives, to endure the bitter ones, and to make the most of the disruptive transitions.

TRUST CANNOT be established simply by saying, "I hear you. I understand. I care." It is not what is said but what is done that allows us to experience a safe, nurturing atmosphere in which love can thrive. It is simply a matter of how lovingly we treat each other.

When we're supported by a growing bond of mutual trust and uncritical acceptance of each other's feelings, self-acceptance grows as well. Whatever we say to each other, we come together as two minds and hearts. With the alternating impact of one imagination on the other, we experience ourselves as defined by the other's picture of us.

"I am your life and you are mine" means shared awareness and shared purpose, but it does not mean giving over responsibility for our lives to someone else, despite our temptation to do so. Love means just the opposite. As one person put it, "I can count on you to care for me only in ways that make me more independent."

One part of loving is learning to get as close to each other as we can without merging.

ONE EXPERIENCE feels good and we hope it will happen again. Another feels bad and we fear it will recur. The direction and intensity of both these positive and negative expectations contribute substantially to our image of what sort of world this is. This image includes the illusion that we can know what to expect. But too high a price is paid for imagining ourselves surer than anyone can be.

We are all excessively hopeful and excessively fearful at times. Exaggerated feelings and unrealistic expectations offer us the illusion of reassurance, but at the cost of needless suffering. If we can keep our need for certainty to a minimum, we won't suffer anymore than is absolutely required by whatever comes next.

Expect the unexpected.

WHAT MUST we do to increase our options for happiness? For one thing, we must give up insisting on an objective reality, since this is no more than a costly escape from our own imagination.

The gateway to the light of personal happiness is a dark passage through the free play of imagination. Until the unimagined aspects of life are allowed to emerge into the light, we remain one-sided characters unprepared for all we dare not imagine.

The same defenses that protect us against suffering deprive us of joy. Suffering must be fully experienced if happiness is to be entirely available. There is no way to play it safe without dulling the pleasure and excitement that life otherwise offers.

If we are to know courage and adventure, the full darkness of whatever we dread must be faced. If we are to realize the full bright glory of our hopes, deep disappointment must be risked.

We should enjoy here while we're here, because there's no here there.

May 25

HEALTHY SEXUALITY is highly underrated. This sounds contradictory, but it's only one of a great many contradictory sexual messages today. For instance, while both men and women openly engage in casual sex, the consequences can be deadly. Also, although we may talk a lot about sex in general, we won't discuss our personal concerns. A great number of people have no idea what healthy sexuality really means, but are too threatened to ask.

Sexuality begins at birth, when you enter your family, community, and culture as a female or male, and it affects your entire life. As John Bradshaw said, "Sexuality is the very core of our being." If we don't feel good about who we are as a man or a woman, the pain can be great—so great, in fact, that sex therapist Sherry Sedgwick sees sex issues among the primary causes of addiction.

What is "normal"? Why are we ashamed of our sexual selves? Why can't we talk about our concerns? Supposedly sexually liberated, we're actually imprisoned by the painful ignorance we must hide.

Openly admitting what we don't know about sex will prove far more rewarding than trying to cover up our inexperience.

AT TIMES our lives get out of control. There will be undeserved troubles, major disappointments, even debilitating illnesses and injuries. If it's not one thing, it's another! Some suffering cannot be helped. Complain as we might about how helpless we feel, that won't work either.

No matter how hard we try to live right, sometimes we will be granted a mess so unmanageable that it seems impossible to endure. But, it can't be helped. No matter how helpless we feel, sorting through suffering to try to transform garbage into something good won't change our lot. There's no use arguing about it. Even if we didn't make the mess, we're the ones who have to clean it up.

Life just keeps coming at you; your only impact is in how you live it.

OUR ANGER is a natural reaction to attack by another person. Some idealistic traditions teach us to aspire to rise above anger. If we try and are unable to transcend our resentment, we often feel inadequate or guilty. And if we are able to ignore our anger, we risk either directing it toward ourselves, taking it out on some innocent third party, or deadening our feelings and burying our other passions along with it.

Anger is sometimes confused with the kind of primitive rage that is uncalled for, destructive, and difficult to contain. This sort of barbaric reaction is an infantile residue that results in violence. More adult anger is an appropriate reaction to mistreatment in the present, directed toward its perpetrator and proportional to its provocation.

As Aristotle wrote, "Anybody can become angry—that is easy; but to be angry with the right person, and to the right degree, and at the right time, and for the right purpose, and in the right way—that is not within everybody's power and is not easy."

Anger isn't bad, but what we do with it can be.

CONVENTIONAL WISDOM admonishes us to face facts and be reasonable. On the surface, it sounds like a good idea, but we need to be cautious. It is by now common knowledge that statistics can be made to lie to support an argument. And even if we were clear about the "facts" of a case, the logical conclusions we derive from them may prove false.

As Martin Luther warned, "Reason is a whore"; that is, it can be made to serve without sincerity in the interests of a later payoff. Facts don't change attitudes and arguments rarely change minds.

If we want to help someone else to discover a better way to live, sometimes all we can do is to try to interest them in how little their present style returns and how much it costs. If their awakening is sufficiently unsettling, then we can offer to stand by their side while they try out new approaches.

Often the best way to lead others is by assuring them that we are right behind them.

May 29

IN INDIA, the training of work elephants begins when they are babies. To keep the elephant calf in place, the trainer ties one of its hind legs to a stake with a rope. The elephant is not yet strong enough to break the rope when the basic instruction is begun.

Advanced training is undertaken when the elephant is full-grown. By then, the beast has become so powerful that when chained to a stake it breaks loose easily and runs off. Wisely, the trainer once again uses a rope to bind the adult elephant.

Although the animal is now strong enough to break loose without difficulty, it does not even try to get away. Apparently convinced by its early experience, the bull elephant perceives the rope as too strong to break.

Unless we replace yesterday's feelings with today's experiences, we will remain bound by the past when we could be free in the present.

WE ALL have plenty to worry about. Past misfortunes can entangle us in anguishing over what we might have done to have made things work out better. Problematic possibilities in the future, no matter how improbable, can consume us in unneeded anxious concerns. There are times when we are wise to rethink the past and to try to anticipate the future. Both tactics can help us to prepare for coping with upcoming problems.

Unfortunately, some people become too immersed in this sort of obsessing. When anyone urges them to stop wasting their precious time worrying, they explain that they understand the wisdom of the advice, but are simply unable to set aside their anxieties about yesterday and tomorrow.

When worries replay in your mind like a broken record, you can't actually force yourself to stop thinking or feeling, but you aren't really helpless to change your focus of attention. You can take the advice of an old Jewish adage, "If you want to forget your other troubles, put a pebble in your shoe." Or you can become actively engaged in doing something constructive for yourself or for someone else.

Worrying can become a way to avoid living.

May 31

IF YOU are not willing to know what you feel, to say what you mean, and to do what you say, then you live as a passive object of fate. However, if you are willing to fully accept, to own, to treasure that which is you, you can transform your fate into your destiny.

To do this, first you have to give up the sentimentality of telling a little bit more than the truth. You have to present yourself first to your own eyes, and when it is safe, to the eyes of others. There is no need to hide your strength, your virtue, your special beauty. Yet all these must be presented within the context of the ordinariness of your weaknesses and your flaws. As William Butler Yeats said, "A soul must become its own betrayer, its own deliverer, the one activity, mirror turned lamp."

What sort of God would make everyone so different and allow only one way for us to serve Him?

IS THERE no end to striving? Even the question is exhausting if we are continually trying to get everything just right instead of simply doing as well as we can. It may not seem like it, but when we insist that everything be just right before we feel really good about it, and so feel really good about ourselves, we are pursuing perfection. Probably it feels just the opposite, as if we are settling for too little, not trying for too much.

When we judge our feelings all good or all bad, we are working, hoping, waiting for everything to be perfect before we feel good enough. It follows that the way we judge ourselves is discouraging. One false move and we feel like failures. Also, our perfectionism is hard on our relationships. To be successful, our marriages must provide enough satisfaction that we won't need anything else.

We want our attachment to whatever we idealize to provide everything we could ever want all the time. This idealistic attitude makes it difficult for us to accept the less-than-perfect, pleasures afforded to ordinary people.

When we stubbornly demand "All or nothing!" life responds, "Very well then, nothing!"

June 2

IN SAMUEL Beckett's play, *Waiting for Godot*, two old clownish tramps come from nowhere in particular and seem to have nowhere in particular to go. So, they wait, and wait, and wait, in the simple sameness of the empty world, no more than a country road, a single tree, and always it is evening, a little late for Godot to show up. Immersed in the boredom of expecting that which does not come, they find that nothing happens, no one comes, and no one goes.

They have defined their existence as a time of waiting for Godot. But who or what is Godot? God? Fate? Meaning, First Principle, Higher Purpose? Perhaps Godot is merely a hopeless name for a nameless hope. What if Godot is nothing? Still, nothing matters except the expected arrival of Godot. So, the characters fill their time with games, play-acting, arguing—distractions from the purposelessness of it all.

To make what we can of the time we have, we must give up asking others, "When will Godot arrive?" and instead ask ourselves, "What are we doing here waiting?"

If we wait to act until we're handed a script, our lives will be one long intermission.

WHEN SOMEONE we love is hurting, in our hearts we hurt too because their suffering matters so much to us. We wish we could make them stop hurting, even if it means taking their place and absorbing their pain. In a way, it's easy to say, "I wish this had happened to me instead of to you," but perhaps that's because there's no chance things will work out that way.

In some situations we can ease the suffering of the ones we love by temporarily assuming some of their responsibilities, by attending to their needs, or by distracting them from their pain. This requires more effort than simply wishing we could take their place and is of more help to our suffering beloved.

But the deepest show of devotion is also the most difficult: accepting our helplessness to alleviate the personal pain of those we love and honoring the intensity of their agony while willingly standing by them and graciously listening to the complaints that their suffering entitles them to express.

Our deepest devotion is often expressed by our willingness to be there to share our loved one's pain.

June 4

WHEN WE are in the midst of trying to change some basic attitudes, we often go through really tough times. Whether our usual posture has been defiant or compliant, impulsive or indecisive, stubbornly opinionated or weakly uncertain, shifting gears is difficult.

Whatever gains we make will be interrupted by backsliding. At times, we will go too far in the opposite direction. There will be periods when we will have let go of old ways without yet getting a firm hold on new ones.

Unless we are patient with ourselves and tolerant of our missteps, we may simply give up on improving things. The support of understanding friends can be a big help.

Changing your ways isn't easy. Accept all the help you can get.

WHEN WE are truly giving to others, we do so without expecting a reward in return. It is gratifying to find that when we are in need, we can count on them to reciprocate. Still, there are other kinds of rewards than receiving in return.

Often, we feel satisfied simply by experiencing the pleasure of having eased their suffering. Also, there may be a ripple effect that is gratification enough. That happens when we give to people in a way that makes them feel sufficiently abundant to provide for others in need, others we may not even know.

The sweetest instance of this chain reaction is in nurturing families. We give to our children without expecting them to respond to us in kind. Instead, knowing the pleasure of having been well cared for, they pass on to their children what they've gotten from us.

However indirectly, what goes around comes around.

June 6

EVEN IN the best of relationships, disputes are inevitable. The only way arguments can be completely avoided is if one partner is chronically accommodating. These arrangements of assigned roles of dominance and submission may be the worst of relationships.

Two autonomous partners are sure to argue at times. During the combat, there may be hostile words, spiteful behavior, and temporary withdrawal, but if we are able to keep in mind that we are fighting with someone we love, our feelings of anger and hurt need not permanently redefine or destroy the relationship.

Even though we are not seeing eye to eye, we can continue to feel heart to heart.

WHAT IF you had been born into another house, another family, would you have been happier? Who knows! But just how happy or unhappy you are with the personality you have and the life you have been dealt is largely a matter of how well you play your cards. It won't help to hope for a reshuffling of the cards, a new hand, or a better deal.

Fighting fate, trying to will what cannot be willed, complaining that life's not fair is useless complaining that simply invites needless suffering.

It's enough to experience the suffering that's absolutely required without whining, "Why me? Why did this have to happen to me?" Complaining can become a way of boasting about how much suffering you can endure.

When problems arise, the only really useful question is, "What do I do now?"

Life isn't fair, but how we react to adversity does make a difference.

June 8

CASUAL SEX in the absence of commitment can be fun for some, but it is not the same thing as making love. As Carl Whitaker commented, "Casual sex is an impersonal date between a penis and a vagina." If you've taken the necessary health precautions, the two of you can remain physically safe, but there's still the risk of emotional danger.

It's very difficult to be sure that each of you stays on the same level of attachment or detachment as the other. One person is likely to believe there is more than physical fun involved and then get hurt. The other may feel guilty and try to make believe he or she feels more affection or love than was ever intended. What happens next is anybody's guess.

Some couples get married out of guilt and end up falling in love. Others move on to other partners apparently without negative emotional consequences. Some find the physical intimacy without the emotional component draining, demoralizing, and ultimately, not as much fun as they thought it would be.

Alliances built on romantic illusions often end up as encounters of the most painful kind.

THERE IS an apocryphal story of a man in Nazi Germany who did nothing the night when he heard the stomping of the storm troopers' jack-boots and the cries of the Jews they had come to persecute. He excused his passivity by explaining, "After all, I am not a Jew."

He remained a noninterventionist when they came for the Catholics, and then again when they came to drag the gypsies away to the concentration camps. On the former occasion, he explained, "After all, I am not a Catholic," and on the latter, "I am not a gypsy."

The night the storm troopers came for him, he complained that when he cried out, nobody came to help him.

If we are not there for others, who will be there for us?

June 10

MIKE TODD described the many ups and downs of his career as a theatrical producer by saying, "I been broke lots of times, but I ain't ever been poor!" The difference between Todd and some inner-city kid is that while both could be destitute, circumstances allowed him to see himself as having a future.

Often, politically and economically oppressed people can only see today. For them, there is no tomorrow much less any day after tomorrow. Release from that sort of trap requires community political action.

But individuals with a wider range of opportunities open to them are trapped sometimes simply because they see themselves as trapped.

In times of desperation our natural hope may be obscured.

WE ALL share certain problems as we develop. The typical outlook of the young is overly optimistic and lacking in compassion, leaving them unprepared for the losses to be faced tomorrow. In contrast, too often, older people can be so consumed with cynicism brought about by yesterday's suffering that they have difficulty enjoying today.

George Santayana said, "The young man who has not wept is a savage, and the old man who will not laugh is a fool."

As we grow up, we have some understanding that we will face disappointments and grow old and, as we age, we can learn, as Martin Buber said, "What a glorious thing it is to grow old in a young way."

The art of growing older without getting old is to retain the youthful joy of being alive.

June 12

SOME PEOPLE appear to be hypersensitive to criticism. They act as if hearing anyone else question how they are doing is too painful to bear.

These same "sensitive" people tend to be overly apologetic and self-denigrating about their own behavior, but then they're easily hurt if anyone else agrees. They complain that the other person is "mean" for not assuring them that they are all right. The subtext of this attitude is their covertly controlling insistence of demanding a constant flow of reassurance from other people.

This kind of touchiness is a subtle form of tyranny, but those around them subjected to it are not required to restrict their own lives. We each have the right to live as we like. The only restriction is that we must not keep others from living as they like. If what we want to say doesn't harm anyone, we can feel free to say it, even if it ruffles some feathers.

 If people are going to be upset no matter what we say, we may as well upset them with the truth.

MANY VIABLE love relationships involve the pairing of opposites. If both partners are overly cautious, they may never do anything adventuresome. If both are exceedingly bold, they may destroy themselves by being recklessly impulsive.

When your partner and you are very different from each other, you can count on each other for those qualities that do not come easily to yourself. Ironically, these same differences that enrich and strengthen your relationship also encourage the recurrent clashes that cause the most pain.

Whatever the content of any couple's quarrels, the differences in their styles usually underlies most arguments. Recognition, acceptance, and a sense of humor about these differences help you make relationships that are lasting, rather than simply chronic.

Mutual hobbies are nice, but a couple's common interest needs to be their relationship.

June 14

THERE ARE many different types of suffering in this life. Having suffered one kind does not necessarily protect us from suffering other kinds as well.

Some people endure disasters of catastrophic illness, multiple losses of loved ones, or continued career failures. Often they expect that having had to undergo calamities of this proportion entitles them to exemption from minor everyday difficulties.

"What more could happen to me?" they implore. Often they feel offended when their seemingly "tragic" situations are made worse by minor mishaps.

Just because you've once been swallowed by a whale doesn't mean you won't also find minnows nibbling at your flanks.

SOME PEOPLE believe in an afterlife; others don't. There's no way for any of us to know for sure until we die. Of the many who've already died, no one ever has ever come back to tell us what it was like.

Everyone is entitled to his or her opinion, but there is some advantage to believing that when you're dead, you're dead, and that's that. Belief in the finality of death helps us to take each moment of life more seriously. If we have only one go-around, we should make the most of it. We are likely to be more attentive to whatever richness we can experience.

Some of us may be tempted to obsess morbidly that there's no point to living, if it's all going to be over someday. There are people who react that way to scientific predictions that our solar system has only a few more million years to survive.

But if we give ourselves a break, we can put our mortality to good use. It can help us avoid procrastinating, being careless, or being inattentive; it can also help us live each day as if it were our last.

Let yourself be enlivened by the imminence of death.

June 16

WHEN YOU find yourself unintentionally repeating some problematic behavior, it usually seems logical to try to do the opposite. For example, if you are chronically late for appointments, you may try to arrive on time, or even to show up early.

When this doesn't work, it's sometimes helpful to shift to the paradoxical approach of freeing yourself from an impulse by indulging it. This trick-against-trick cure is like "setting a thief to catch a thief." Just as one poison may cure another, a thorn in the skin can be removed by using another thorn.

Decide to arrive late for your next appointment. Try doing on purpose whatever it is you usually do unintentionally.

Once we know what it feels like to do something on purpose, we become better able to stop doing it unintentionally.

WHEN WE have a case of the blues, we're likely to make things worse by telling ourselves that if we feel this bad, we must have done something wrong. Life seems awful and it's all our own fault.

If you're embedded deeply enough in a truly bad mood, it's hard to see over the edge. One part of you says things will brighten up after a while. Another part answers, "Yeah, but so what!" Too often, the cynical side deflates whatever hope we can muster.

If you're wise enough, you may recognize that when your depression lifts you'll feel better. If you're too overwhelmed for even that, it often helps to give at least some shape or form to your present plight by acknowledging it to yourself: "I'm so overwhelmed . . . or depressed . . . or scared . . . or sad . . . to see any end to this." Then sometimes all you can do is endure your present misery and wait for a break in your emotional fog.

The blues ain't nothin' but a good soul feelin' bad.

June 18

A COUPLE may be well matched in their overall emotional and intellectual development, but most likely, one will be stronger than the other in some areas and vice versa. Common sense tells us that when there's something to be decided on or dealt with that requires special knowledge or aptitude, the partner who is best prepared should prevail.

Unfortunately, these situations can be difficult and cause discord, since the evident strength versus weakness position leads to a power struggle that doesn't make much sense. Often it is the underdog who is most stubbornly dug in.

Like it or not, when your mate and you are in a power struggle, it is the older child of the two of you who must give in.

THERE ARE periods in each of our lives when we become so consumed with worry about a crisis, it's almost impossible to concentrate on anything that makes us feel better or to carry out any productive activities that might offer a sense of accomplishment. The harder we work at trying to escape our anxiety, the more tightly it ties us down.

One way we can disentangle ourselves from this web of worry is to take it on intentionally. Set your alarm half an hour early, get up, and give all of your attention to the anxiety you've been trying to avoid. Once you take charge of scheduling a set time for your worries, the less likely they are to come upon you unexpectedly. Worrying on schedule helps you focus your thinking and manage your time.

If you don't want your worries to hit you from behind, face them up front.

June 20

A FOLKTALE tells of a man sentenced to death who talked the king into giving him a reprieve. He assured the king that within one year, he would teach the king's horse how to fly. If he failed, the man said, he would be willing to be put to death at the end of the year.

Asked why he would make this bizarre deal with the king, the man explained, "Within a year the king may die, or I may die, or the horse may die. Furthermore, in a year, who knows? Maybe the horse will learn how to fly."

Some of us are typically reckless. Others are chronically cautious. To avoid either extreme, we must learn to ask ourselves, What is the worst that can happen? What is the best we can hope for? What is the most likely eventuality?

Unless we learn to recognize risk in personal terms, we sacrifice both the options of reasonable safety and excitement.

Every decision involves risk.

ALTHOUGH THERE are rare and wonderful occasions when strangers connect with each other almost immediately, most of us find that getting to know each other is more difficult. Whatever the chemistry between two people who have just met, developing a truly personal relationship takes time.

Time is necessary, but it is not sufficient. Some people meet often, spend long periods together, and never get any closer than when they first met. "We've talked together every Friday for six months," may really mean, "We've had one talk twenty-four times."

If we want to get to know what other people are like inside, it's often necessary to risk revealing ourselves before they are willing to do the same. Yet, many of us avoid showing our neediness without first feeling reassured that the other person can be trusted.

There's nothing wrong with beginning a relationship in a way that allows both of you to feel safe. One way is to establish caring connections on grounds that are personal, but still allow your secret self to stay safely hidden.

If you want to make a friend, ask a favor.
—Chinese proverb

June 22

WHEN WE experience anxiety, we almost always wish we didn't. Often we are tempted to try to shake off our uneasiness by denial or distraction, but this dismissal can be a serious mistake. Unless we are irrationally afraid of something that isn't actually dangerous, a modest amount of anxiety can alert us to signs of imminent danger that would otherwise cause us needless harm.

Moderate anxiety can also motivate us to call on resources we otherwise allow to lie dormant. For some emotionally conservative people, anxiety is the only access they have to their suppressed excitement.

In any case, none of us ever feels fully prepared for totally new undertakings. Some anxiety is simply the necessary uneasiness that comes with undertaking new adventures.

Anxiety can be useful to motivate us for change.

IN LONG-TERM love relationships, we get to know how our partners react to some of the things we characteristically say and do. Our arguments become a ritual dance in which we both keep repeating the same dumb steps. We get to recognize some of the ways we criticize each other, or rebut the other's criticism of us.

After yet another go-around, we each promise ourselves, "I'll never do that again!" A short time later, we find ourselves astonished when our ears hear our mouths spouting the same stupid stuff.

It may be worthwhile to say "I'm sorry" to the loved one we've wronged, but when it comes to the characteristic style with which we defend our hurt feelings, there's no use swearing that we'll never do it again. We're better off admitting that, though we take responsibility for our words, we can't always control what we say, asking our partners to help us recognize what we're doing the next time it comes up.

Love isn't just saying you're sorry. It's also trying to avoid repeating whatever you were sorry for.

June 24

WHETHER OUR pain is physical or emotional, most of us find it easiest to bear when we believe there is hope of it ending. The tension that arises out of our stubborn attempt to fight off the intractable aching in our bodies or souls only serves to increase the intensity of our anguish. Once we accept that we must live with some pain all of our lives, we are free to give our hurt no more attention than it absolutely warrants.

There are some bouts of the flu that make us feel as if we are dying. Someone once compared living through a prolonged, severe case of the flu with the experience of an addict suffering the withdrawal symptoms of kicking a drug habit cold turkey. The similarity may have been exaggerated, but the difference is crucial and illustrates one reason why a drug habit is so hard to break. Addicts know that they can end the pain with a chemical fix—no matter how much longer it extends the misery of their addiction. The flu patients have no way out, and so resign themselves to their suffering until time heals their hurting.

Putting up with pain protects us from increasing it.

SOME LOSS of love is inevitable. One way or another, every love relationship ends. In long-lasting loves, it may be no more than the matter of who dies first. In some friendships, one partner simply outgrows the other. Even in the best and most enduring kinds of caring, every so often discord disrupts the comfortable closeness. During those messes, it's difficult to remember how much someone else matters to us.

We all know that the better it feels to be close to someone, the worse it is when we feel apart. Some people are so frightened of being abandoned they'll do almost anything to avoid facing the pain of loss. To play it safe, they sacrifice whatever closeness they might enjoy by keeping their distance. If there is even a hint that the beloved may be backing off, rather than risk being deserted, they scuttle the relationship.

Having no love to lose is a safe, sad way of living.

June 26

MOST PEOPLE would agree that having friends is worthwhile. Few will concede that it is also important to have enemies.

Friends afford us the pleasure of their company, some support when we feel needy, a soothing sense that we are part of a community, and they are likely to put in a good word when our name comes up among strangers.

When our day-to-day actions and attitudes involve a low-keyed amenability aimed at pleasing others, we are likely to acquire many acquaintances—a few of whom may become our friends. If instead, we express our personal thoughts and feelings openly, we are more likely to polarize those who do take notice—some of whom will become close friends and a few of whom will disapprove strongly enough to become our enemies.

Whichever of these modes we choose will be insignificant to most people. There are some people I would be embarrassed to have as friends. The enmity of people whose attitudes I find off-putting attests to the differences in our outlooks. I would prefer that if they spoke of me to strangers, that they would make clear their disapproval of my beliefs.

We all need friends, and enemies, too.

FEELING BORED can be an interesting experience. The ten thousand things that make up our experience each day are neither intrinsically interesting nor uninteresting. The same things that interest us one day can bore us the next, and vice versa.

There is some evidence that continuing to do the same things in the same way may encourage us to lose interest. But what about those times when nothing seems of interest?

One way we can restore our enthusiasm about a life that has lost its allure is to ask ourselves, "Why am I bored right now? What is going on within me that has so sapped my interest that I feel apathetic about the world around me?"

Even if we can't come up with an answer to our questions, at least we will have allowed our boredom to arouse our interest.

Boredom can become interesting if only we pay attention to it.

June 28

MANY OF us worry a lot about why it's sometimes so hard to get along with other people. When two of us interact we often experience what goes on in such different ways that it's a wonder we get along well as often as we do. Sometimes there are such great disparities in our points of view that if either of us could see things through the other's eyes each of our visions of our relationship would make no sense at all.

Perhaps we worry too much about what went wrong and take too little time trying to identify what it was that worked so well. It's tempting to take satisfying interactions for granted, rather than risk disrupting them by exploring what we might be doing that contributes to these lovely moments.

In any case, we are better off experiencing relationships than analyzing them. But if we are going to devote some energy to solving problems in our relationships, it might serve us well to give at least equal time to examining what it is that sometimes makes our being together such a wonderful experience.

If it's not broken, don't fix it; but do take a look at what makes it work so well.

OFTEN GUILT is the bad feeling we get when we've done something wrong. Although it may originate out of a fear of punishment for not following others' dictates, guilt can be developed as a touchstone for judging whether or not we are living up to our own ethical standards.

If we don't wallow in our guilt, it may motivate us to atone for our misconduct, either by making amends or by trying to compensate for our missteps with some particularly worthwhile undertaking.

We can begin by examining our guilt. Do we feel that what we've done was truly wrong? Have we really hurt someone else, or are we simply worried that they would disapprove?

When our guilt arises out of a sin of omission—not having fulfilled someone else's expectation—it requires especially careful examination. Often this sort of guilt turns out to be no more than resentment about unfair or unwanted obligations—resentment we have suppressed and turned on ourselves. When we recognize this, we are better able to shrug off both the guilt and the imposed obligations.

Guilt can be good for us.

June 30

WE SOMETIMES complain that somebody else is driving us crazy, but this can't happen unless we're captive victims in an inescapable, destructive environment, such as infants in dysfunctional families or prisoners-of-war in brainwashing programs. Regardless of how obnoxious another person may seem, we don't have to react by emotionally coming apart at the seams. However, if the other person has some political power over us, we may have tough decisions to make, such as confrontations that risk our possibilities for promotion or even losing our jobs.

Most of the time when we complain that the attitudes and behavior of our boss or co-worker are terribly annoying, we are overlooking our own contribution to how unhappy we feel. The missing piece is how we react to the unpleasantness they create.

We have many alternatives besides going crazy. Of our various options, the only one that makes no sense at all is holding someone else responsible for the misery created by our own reactions.

How we react to stress is our own responsibility.

3

WHO AM I IN MY WORLD?

If I am not for myself, who will be for me?
And if I am for myself only, what am I?
— RABBI HILLEL

What the gurus know that the seekers do not
is that we are all pilgrims.
— SHELDON KOPP

July 1

"WHO AM I in my world?" may be one of the most difficult questions to answer. We have to attain perspective of ourselves to discover our own uniqueness. For one thing, we need to listen attentively to others around us to learn who we are that they aren't. And we must listen for the echoes from the depths of our own souls, the resonant vibrations that give voice to our authentic, God-given self, our own divine spark, our connection with the Higher Power.

Listening is not the only thing we have to do, but it very well may be the most difficult. A Zen story tells of a master instructing three young students to spend time in total silence. "You may not speak a word," he said, "from this moment on."

"I shall not speak at all," said the first.

"How stupid! Why did you talk?" asked the second.

"I am the only one who hasn't spoken," said the third.

In silence you can hear your inner voice telling you the truth.

Do I have value as a human being? Does my worth depend on what I have done or on who I am? Both are aspects of self-esteem. As children, we were given many messages about ourselves, some good, some bad, but being shamed by our parents had the most damaging effect on how we felt about ourselves. Shaming is worse than being told that you did something wrong; it is being told that you are a bad person. A parent may say, "Look how stupid, foolish, clumsy . . . you are! You should be ashamed of yourself!"

Because we were too young to doubt our parents, repeated exposure to this kind of abuse evoked an inner echo of self-contempt that often continues throughout our lives. "If only I tried harder, I could . . ." becomes the enduring admonition of our own inner voice. Beyond the edge of awareness are the drive, the longing, and the lingering hope of being good enough to be validated by our parents.

Those of us who suffer a persistent sense of shame need to learn to forgive ourselves for not being perfect, for only being human. Knowing that no one can be perfect is not enough. Before we give up trying to achieve the impossible, we must also feel in our hearts what we know in our heads.

We must learn to forgive ourselves again and again and again.

July 3

WE MAKE a mistake if we ask ourselves, "Am I good enough?" or "Is it worthwhile to be me?" Whoever we are or whatever we do is who and what we are supposed to be.

Many of our doubts began when we were children, and someone led us to question the worth of our existence or performance. But whoever heard of a baby who was inadequate, or a child who did not know just exactly how to be a child? How could it not be all right for me to be me? How could it not be just right for you to be you?

Unfortunately, we weren't old enough, or for some other reason, we were not yet capable of considering the anger, the fear, and the judgments that have caused us to doubt ourselves ever since. The greatest mistake we could make now would be to carry on as if we didn't know better by living a life defined by someone else.

No matter what anyone else says, we've got to be who we are.

THE DIFFERENCES between the Western Judeo-Christian traditions and their Oriental Hindu-Buddhist counterparts can be understood in part as the contrast between a straight line and a circle. In the West, the straight line represents the path we are to follow so we can improve ourselves, from a beginning point as a flawed human being, extending an awesome, infinite distance to the never-to-be-reached perfection.

In the circular way of the Orient, we need only to recognize that each of us is already the Buddha. In other words, we need only to surrender to our true nature. As we find ways to give up the struggle to change who we are, we free ourselves from the bondage of trying to be what we are not. All that separates us from the bliss of nirvana is the maya of illusion.

There is wisdom in both traditions, if we understand each to mean "How good am I at being myself?"

Victory lies in surrender to oneself.

July 5

ONE OF the ways that grown-ups take care of children is by telling them fairy tales. The pretend atmosphere of fairy tales shelters children from the overwhelming uncertainties and the confusing sense of helplessness that adults must face from time to time. No matter how scary or violent the tale is, the struggle between good and evil is always clear and good always triumphs in the end. Also, the difference is clear between courage and cowardice, justice and injustice, help and hindrance.

Even though grown-ups are trying to take care of their children by making up stories, when we become adults, we have to give up the fairy tales our parents told us. Desperately holding onto the vision of a life in which the face of the enemy is clear and the good guys always win, we waste our lives waiting for the happy ending.

What makes life's pain seem so unbearable is the mistaken belief that we can avoid it somehow.

MOST OF us do our best to avoid discovering that we are only ordinary people, living in an indifferent world that has no conclusions for our randomly ordered lives. The harder we try to maintain the opposite, the more we fail to see how our illusions contribute to the problems we have. Mistakenly, we view ourselves as helpless victims of our pasts. Paradoxically, at the same time, we envision ourselves becoming the triumphant, powerful masters of our futures.

Living life as the ordinary people we turn out to be, we must eventually accept the shifting ambiguities of being both good and bad, wise and foolish, fortunate and unfortunate. Then comes a lifelong search to answer such questions as, "How can we depend on each other without expecting to be taken care of? When is it wise to trust the other, with what, and how much? What is the best way for us to manage our finally unmanageable lives?"

The tension between certainty and doubt propels us forward.

July 7

IN *CATCH-22*, Joseph Heller humorously illustrated the double bind in a military setting: Being crazy excused you from active duty, but if you turned yourself in for mental illness, you were considered too sane to be exempt. In any context a double bind is frustrating, but when someone you love or depend on imposes contradictory demands, you're in a very personal no-win situation.

The double bind could begin with a statement like "If you will pretend to be who I want you to be, I will reward you." Or it may be "If only you will pretend to stop being the person you are, I will reward you." The catch-22 comes with a second statement that always accompanies the first: "Pretend that you are not pretending."

To get out of a double bind requires first that you recognize you're in it. Then you have to communicate this understanding to the person who set up the rules to this game, along with the message that you won't play.

Control is an illusion.

FREQUENTLY, PEOPLE who find their adult problems unmanageable were raised in families where being hypocritical was not an exception but a family rule. What they had been taught to believe in was totally contradicted by what was really going on. When illusion falls away to reveal lies that the family lives, the children feel unsafe and untrusting for a long, long time.

Needing to protect themselves, children come to depend on self-restricting, fantasy-bound, risk-avoiding attitudes and behaviors. Their original innocence is transformed into what Rollo May calls "pseudoinnocence." This denies feelings of hopelessness, makes the pain of disappointment more bearable, and brings a false sense of order to a chaotic life.

There may have been little else that we, as children, could have done at the time, but out of a life like this, we may gradually develop neurotic ways that continue into adulthood. One of the most restricting fantasies we're stuck with is thinking that if only we can be really good, surely someone will take care of us.

None of us is who we were taught we are supposed to be.

July 9

AS IN theater, the power of pretending can move the audience to sympathy, anger, grief, and relief. If pretending can call forth such powerful responses in free agents who have merely stopped by for a few hours of entertainment, we can only begin to imagine what it may evoke in someone who grows up trapped in a setting where family members only pretend to be what they seem.

Our perception and understanding are determined to a significant degree by the unconscious forms our imagination imposes on every experience. Whether or not we are aware of it, when we enter into a relationship we each bring preconceived ways of thinking and reacting. However, if together we become aware of each other's hidden ploys, then our mutual, expanding consciousness can shift the scene. In other words, if both of us realize that you have become a player in my personal drama and I have become a player in yours, then we can collaborate to work out new and original stories.

We can avoid replaying our powerful past by distinguishing clearly between past, present, and future.

WHAT ARE we to do when we must decide between the loneliness of independence and the self-sacrifice of conformity? There are times when the only options that seem available to us are either to suffer the seemingly unbearable isolation of standing alone, or to savor the sweet comfort of certainty by surrendering and becoming a part of the herd.

No one is beyond such temptations. Even Solzhenitsyn, the expatriate Soviet writer whose life has become a symbol of an individualistic spirit, admits having seen the options and been tempted. "I remember very well . . ." he wrote in *The Gulag Archipelago*, "that I experienced the happiness of simplification . . . not having to think things through; the happiness of being immersed in the life everyone else lived."

We remain both graced and burdened when we continue to recognize that people choose different courses of action not because they are better or worse than we are but because they understand the options differently than we do.

To be creative we must follow a path of our own. When we are lost, we must find our own way home.

WHEN PARENTS tell children fairy tales about life, they're usually hoping to protect them. But, as children grow older and notice contradictions, too often parents insist that the family must go on pretending that they aren't pretending.

By adolescence, children are confused, realizing that their parents can't be trusted to tell the truth, and yet they are still too helpless and bewildered to try to take on a world that makes no sense.

In desperate attempts to protect ourselves from overwhelming vulnerability, we sometimes create myths of our own about who we are and how the world should work. The problem is that this kind of fantasizing doubles our misery. We add the avoidable disappointment of the eventual shattering of our illusions to the necessary pain of confronting the real world.

Reality may be painful, but shattered illusions can hurt even more.

IT'S TEMPTING at times to wait for someone outside ourselves to bring meaning to our lives. For some people, their central longing seems to be for someone who *really* cares. Such people do not focus clearly on whether how they live is good for them and makes them happy. They pay less attention to how other people actually treat them than to pursuing that someone who will *really* love them.

The question to be asked is, "How would we ever know if someone really cared?" Wouldn't it be better to be treated well by people who might not *really* care than to be treated badly by those who assured us that they did? We will never know for sure how others feel about us, but we can certainly tell how we are being treated.

Searching for certainty to be something to someone else limits our chance to become who we are to ourselves.

If we wait for someone to really love us, we may never learn how to love anyone else.

OFTEN WE see ourselves as successful human beings because we succeed at something. The problem is that when our efforts fail, we define ourselves as failures. At such times we are likely to lose out on the self-esteem to which we're entitled because of our honest efforts to do things right.

Our need for mastery and certainty tempts us to categorize our actions and attitudes as either good or bad, wise or foolish, adequate or inadequate. Our moods change accordingly, so we're continuously on a roller-coaster ride of inflated highs and exaggerated lows.

When we lose interest in categorizing our efforts, we'll be relieved to give up the double-entry bookkeeping of gold stars and demerits. And if there is an angel at the gate of heaven, it's doubtful that we would be asked, "How often did you get it right?" More likely, the question would be, "Did you do as well as you could?"

If God can forgive our imperfections, who are we not to forgive ourselves?

IN THE classic tragic plays, the good people fall from grace. Fate draws the hero (or heroine) toward an awful end because of some tragic flaw of character. Most often, the fatal weakness is an excess of some virtue, such as pride or determination.

Many of us are similar in that we see ourselves as especially selected victims of cruel fate. We suffer, it seems, of necessity, by being committed to some higher value, some creative force. Lacking perspective and humor, we take our situations too seriously and the absurdity of life not seriously enough. In a self-fulfilling prophesy, we participate in our own unhappy dramas, feeling that we do so through no real fault of our own.

Our confusion is understandable, because our excess of virtue has become a vice. It may be anger, sexual longing, pride, or the craving for power that began naturally, grew out of proportion, and ended up being destructive.

We insist that our situation is special, because it's so hard to accept how ordinary we all are.

July 15

FRUSTRATION, PAIN, and disappointment are part of the nature of life, but it is neither natural nor necessary to elevate the universal, everyday bits of unhappiness to the tragic extreme of hysterical misery. When people stubbornly insist that they were dealt more than their share or that somehow they have been especially selected as victims of cruel fate, they insist on seeing themselves as heroic.

Probably they were faced too early and too often with more pressure and less caring than they could endure. "But I had an unhappy childhood" is a current, popular excuse. That may have been true, but what is the cause of misery now? Unwillingness to change? If so, then the smug superiority of tragic heroism really cannot be distinguished from common spitefulness and a life lived with this attitude prevailing becomes a good example of solutions that don't serve us well.

An unhappy childhood may be a good reason for starting out badly, but it's a poor excuse for continuing to live that way.

WHEN YOU are under stress, your hidden self may appear any time your conscious sentinels of reason and consistency are not on duty. Like an illegitimate child who confronts a denying parent, at an unguarded moment your disowned self may seize the opportunity to claim its rightful place in your life.

One time or another, everyone's hidden thoughts are unintentionally revealed by a slip of the tongue. Embarrassment is softened by resorting quickly to parlor psychoanalysis, discounting the exposure as no more than a familiar instance of the universal fallibility of human nature. "A Freudian slip," we reassure each other, colluding to make no more of it.

Encountering this evidence of your shadow self may seem forboding. It will serve you well to remember that your shadow side is not all forbidden, evil impulses but simply a collection of all the personal characteristics that your conscious personality cannot acknowledge.

If God knows everything, what is there to hide?

July 17

INEVITABLY, OUR natural spontaneity is interrupted by our parents. Sometimes this is necessary for our safety and sometimes the reasons are merely pragmatic. In any case, as our range of spontaneous behaviors gets narrower and narrower, our sense of self-worth suffers. Acceptance encourages a feeling of being worthwhile. Punishment and threat induce the opposite.

In the interest of self-protection, we learn early how to preempt punishment by developing a sense of guilt. However, when guilt causes sufficient anxiety, we have to repress even the thought of having unacceptable impulses, so we end up acting like wind-up toys, caricatures of self-control.

While we insist that we are simply being "reasonable," it is very obvious to other people just how dogmatic and stubbornly opinionated we really are.

The illusion of power over our own or another's feelings is not a paper tiger; it is a deadly dragon.

WHEN WE remain unduly attached to our childhood, our nostalgia centers around a wish to make things work out right once and for all. Self-absorbed and petulant, we insist on the right to an unpromised rose garden or restitution for our accident of birth.

Feeling ourselves to be the heroes or heroines of yet uncompleted fairy tales, we refuse to believe that the villains who have disappointed us will go unpunished or that we'll never get the compensation we deserve.

Those of us who are caught up in these romantic fantasies go on insisting that there must be someone who will mend our broken childhood dreams. In our search for a magic helper, some of us become psychotherapy patients. A few of us even presume that we ourselves can bestow the magic helpers and so become professional helpers. There are hazards to either course.

Each image of ourselves is misleading because it is incomplete.

July 19

THE IMPOSSIBLE chore of making sure that everything is perfect, including ourselves, makes us procrastinate about everything we do. Adding indecisiveness to our paralysis, we try to resolve unanswerable questions before we risk doing the wrong thing. "What is reasonable, fair, normal, and right?" we waste our time asking. Unrelenting ruminations and abstract worries keep us out of more active trouble and allow us the reassuring illusion that we are above the muddle of everyday irritations and disappointments, but still, we live our lives threatened and anxious about losing control.

The more we can learn to choose the free pleasure of a life that combines the seeming contradictions of self-discipline and self-indulgence, systematic thought and irrational feeling, reasonable caution and exciting adventure, the more manageable life becomes in reality. Accepting the eternal oppositions within ourselves is far more fun than soberly pursuing a life of controlled consistency.

We will all be fools at times. When we accept that, our imagination opens to possibilities we were once too wise to consider.

SHAME HAS long been misunderstood. Embarrassment is not shame, and also shame is not guilt.

Guilt is the anxiety that goes with something you've done that you believe is wrong. Shame is the anxiety over disapproval that you have failed to meet certain ego ideals. Shame is a learned piece of personal pathology, having to do with unfulfilled expectations. Instead of being rooted in situations of the moment, shame is centered in a person's overall appraisal of what he or she is worth as a human being. The stakes are exorbitantly high because shame carries with it the threats of abandonment, loss of love, and ultimate emotional starvation.

Feeling ashamed of ourselves when we make a mistake or do something foolish means that we have a low regard for our own self-worth. Blaming our parents for whatever they did to create our sense of shame is easy, but it is also irrelevant. You and your feelings are your responsibility now.

What you think of yourself is up to you.

July 21

YOU MAY successfully keep some parts of yourself hidden in the dark, but you will not be able to avoid casting that shadow onto others around you. Projecting your shadow happens when you encounter something in someone else and your reaction is out of proportion. "How could anyone act like that?" you think; or "My God, that's weird! People like that should be locked up!"

Even though the thought of such behavior makes you feel awful, somehow you simply cannot stop thinking about it. Again and again, you reassure yourself that *you* would not possibly do anything like that.

Whenever you find yourself feeling self-righteously drawn or compelled to judge another's personality or behavior, you are in the midst of such a projection. The negative feelings you have about your hidden self have been projected onto the other person.

The stranger and the enemy are mirrored reflections of your unrecognized self.

OFTEN WHEN movie stars are interviewed, they will say, "I'm really a very shy person." The contrast between their very public career and their personal claim seems so drastic that their comments are hard to believe. They may or may not be who they claim, but it is possible that normally, they are genuinely shy.

Some people are innately reserved in their manner, naturally more comfortable with the inner world of private experiences. They may have a well-developed sense of self and understand that when they feel embarrassed it is the external situation, rather than some defect in their own character. They may also realize that many other people are also this way.

If shyness makes you miserable, a sense of shame may be behind your needless suffering. But if you simply accept feeling different from those who aren't shy, it's possible to enjoy solitude without feeling lonely. Shyness can reflect a deep sense of shame or simply a natural preference for solitude. The former hangs like a dark cloud over your life. The latter feels like a fresh spring shower.

When we honor our peculiarities, we can make the most of all the singular things we are.

July 23

LEARNING TO accept responsibility for taking care of ourselves is one of the most difficult tasks in life. When we were very young, we needed protection, and hopefully our parents provided it. However, this expectation of caretaking, appropriate then, may be the source of later problems.

As we grew older, many of us assigned our parents the added responsibility for our emotional well-being. If we were sad, we expected them to cheer us up. If we were angry, we counted on them to fix whatever caused us to be upset. Unfortunately, when our parents weren't around or wouldn't perform this service any longer, instead of taking care of ourselves, we looked for the closest substitute.

Believing in the fantasy that someone else is responsible for your feelings gives you the luxury of someone to blame, but blame implies that the other person is in charge and leaves you feeling weak and "one-down." Life without this illusion will not save you from experiencing pain, but when you do, you'll have an opportunity to gain from it.

 Nietzsche said, "That which doesn't kill me makes me stronger."

THERE'S A vast difference between feeling guilty about what I do and feeling ashamed of who I am. I can change what I do, but how am I going to change who I am?

I may feel guilty when I choose to do something that is not permitted—when I lie or cheat. If I do something wrong, I have the possibility of being a worthwhile person who has done a bad thing. Shame, on the other hand, is an overwhelming experience, implying that I'm basically inadequate, making me feel like I need to cover up.

To complicate matters, I may feel guilty about being ashamed of something I've done. Or I may have a secret sense of pride for being better than others who don't have the good sense to feel guilty. Then I may feel ashamed at having been pleased with myself for feeling pleasure over a petty moral victory.

The tricks of the imagination are beyond counting. That's part of why it's so difficult to live a sensible life.

There's no need to create any more misery than life already requires.

July 25

IN *The Picture of Dorian Gray*, Oscar Wilde illustrates a personality split between an insensitively detached public image and an excruciatingly vulnerable private vision. The decadence espoused by Wilde in his own life turns out to be a pathetically insistent denial used to protect himself from being overwhelmed by the anguish of his underlying disillusionment.

Dorian Gray is a physically beautiful man, fully committed to passionate self-absorption, blatantly caring nothing for anyone else. After a life of ever-deepening degradation, he tries to change his ways. But, his inability to maintain a unified self has resulted in his empty, soulless life. Divided, he is his own enemy. Ultimately, he destroys himself.

The story offers each of us an opportunity to wonder how far apart our own private selves are from our public images. And if we never reconcile the two, we do not act in harmony with our innermost selves. How then do we expect to find meaning in life?

Whatever we believe about ourselves, the opposite is also true.

MUCH OF our time is taken up with mundane maintenance chores. Most of the rest is filled with doubt and
contradictions. Whether or not we deny it, more often
than we wish, we are uncertain and afraid.

It's only life! We can face our feelings or we can
create a fantasy. Without justifying or explaining, we
can simply deny whatever challenges the fairy tale
vision of our selves. To accomplish this, we may have
to disavow whole experiences. Getting really carried
away, we could completely dissociate those episodes
that contradict our story. The extreme example of this
is Dr. Jekyll and his alter ego, Mr. Hyde.

Another reason we might want to create a fantasy is
the perception that it will protect us from our own
pain. As one woman said, "I need to fit perfectly into
someone else's mold. Otherwise, I experience all my
own feelings."

*Avoiding our feelings can cause more pain than
facing them.*

July 27

A RELATIVELY new consideration for many of us is the other-sex aspects of our personalities. For so long, men and women had to fit the stereotype for their gender or suffer harsh judgment from their parents and peers. To compensate for imagined flaws in their sexual identities, they developed extravagant postures as swaggering, macho males or helpless, faint-hearted females. The more each exaggerated, the more desperately dependent and ruthlessly manipulative they became with one another. On their own, both Rhett Butler and Scarlett O'Hara are incomplete. Whatever the cost, they must have each other.

Once we learn to accept that each of us has both masculine and feminine traits, we can relax both within ourselves and in our relationships with the opposite sex. For some of us, this acceptance is a very difficult core change. But at the end of the passage to acceptance of ourselves, our reward is personal freedom. What a relief to acknowledge that masculine men can be both tough and tender, and that feminine women can be both soft and strong.

If you feel you have something to prove, you probably also feel there's something to hide.

WHAT WOULD you choose for your epitaph? "She took good care of others"? "He did his best"? In high school, your English teacher may have asked you to write a theme on this so you'd give some thought to the direction of your life.

In thinking about how you would sum up your life now, what if you discovered that you are living your life in a style set up primarily to prove to others that you deserve to have that epitaph? Many people seem to be focused on the results of what they are doing—to be good enough, or to achieve enough. Their anxiety about the outcome makes them miss out on enjoying the experience of who they are instead of who they think they should be.

Death comes to all of us, but the extent that we are our own person is measured by how much we have lived our own lives. With both life and death, the best way is your own way.

We are free to choose what sort of lives we'll live.

July 29

IN *Necessary Losses*, Judith Viorst writes, "Parents unconsciously use and misuse their children. Do well. Make me proud. Don't aggravate me. The unspoken deal is this: If you will bury the parts I don't like, then I will love you. The unspoken choice is this: Lose yourself or lose me."

When family rules from our childhood carry over to adult love relationships, often they translate into attitudes such as, "When I'm upset, you're wrong!" If you are the one usurping the power, taking the position as parent, your mate is apt to retaliate just as a child might, by withdrawing or rebelling. There are many adult versions of these behaviors. For example, when we're unable to get our own way, we may settle for trying to prevent others from getting their way.

Whether you're the one blaming or you're the one protecting yourself, it's helpful to wonder why you are not acting or reacting in loving ways with someone you love. Usually, you'll find that the bottom line is fear—fear of losing yourself, the other's love, or both.

When we run scared, our capacity for love is limited.

IN HINDU mythology, every great rotating circle of time is an inevitable and repeated sequence of the four world ages. In each cycle, the universe is created in perfect order, only to fall into renewed disorder.

In the first age, the newly created universe sits squarely on four legs. It is a sweet and easy, dependable time. Everything seems to go right and life seems to make sense. In the second age, life loses one of its legs, and now preserving balance is harder to do. Kindness calls for conscious effort. Duty and devotion no longer come naturally. Next comes the stage where life is tottering on two legs, increasingly unstable. Self-confidence and high ideals give way to panicky, mean-spirited grabbing for whatever we can get. Paradoxically, our opportunistic struggle to survive ushers in the next and still darker age. We lose it all and there is only the absolute awfulness of everything—total degradation when we are all at our worst. Life is totally disrupted.

The Hindu myths help us understand that life will continue to be a mixture of easy living disrupted by hard times. That's just the way it is.

It's harder to be loving when you're losing.

A SUFI story tells of a time when Nasrudin ferried an eminent scholar across a turbulent river. As a way of distracting himself from his fears as they passed through some particularly rough water, the academic pointed out that the ferryman had spoken incorrectly. He asked Nasrudin if he had ever studied grammar. When the mulla replied that he had not, the pedant commented critically, "Then half your life has been wasted."

Minutes later, the currents grew dangerously stronger. Nasrudin asked his well-educated passenger if he had ever learned to swim. The scholar admitted that indeed he had not. Sighing, Nasrudin said wryly, "Then all of your life has been wasted. The ferryboat is sinking!"

Power and powerlessness depend on the situation.

A FOURTEENTH-CENTURY Dominican was charged with mystical heresy. Meister Eckhart had to defend his beliefs that God is love and that personal salvation, the center of life, can only be sought by direct union with God—a union that could be achieved only by facing God with unswerving affection. He also believed that "however you accomplish this is the way for you." A legend tells of Meister Eckhart meeting a beautiful naked boy and asking where he comes from:

> *"I've come from God."*
> *"Where did you leave him?"*
> *"In virtuous hearts."*
> *"Who are you?"*
> *"A king."*
> *"Where is your kingdom?"*
> *"In my heart. . . ."*
> *And he disappeared.*
> *For it was God himself—*
> *Who was having a bit of fun.*

God is a stand-up comic with an audience who seldom appreciates His sense of humor.

August 2

EVERY SELF is divided and each includes contradictions that can never be settled once and for all. The opposing aspects of our personalities remain in an uneasy state of tension.

Within every one of us, there are the polarities of masculinity and femininity, reason and imagination, and individual needs and a sense of social responsibility. In addition, we have to come to terms with simultaneously possessing both higher spiritual consciousness and base biological instincts.

These dilemmas are too troubling to be faced head-on all the time. Fortunately, self-awareness fluctuates enough for us to periodically escape the strain of coping with so much internal contradiction.

Still, we eventually have to get a clear concept of who we are or we will never feel in charge of ourselves.

We cannot do what can't be done, but still we must do what we can.

YOUR EMERGING awareness of your self required that you learn when and how and to whom it was appropriate to reveal that self. Some expressions of feeling had to be hidden and others had to be faked if you were to gain approval and avoid disapproval. You had to be the person that *they* expected you to be. You had to learn the doctrine of the mask, that is, how to develop your compliant false self.

At the time when your self-confidence and self-esteem depended largely on your success in meeting external standards, you responded to your self as you saw others responding to you. You knew you had a self, but you were not yet sure just what that self was all about. It was necessary to hide your own identity behind a pose that would protect it from the punishment and humiliation that sometimes accompanied other people's disapproval. For a while it was necessary, but eventually the lifelong process of self-definition had to begin—otherwise how would you distinguish the "me" from the "not-me"?

Who are you . . . really?

August 4

IF YOU haven't been through a depression, it's probably hard to believe recoverers when they say they were lucky to have had the experience.

It is hard for those who haven't been addicted and then begun true recovery to understand what these recovering people mean when they call themselves lucky. They laugh freely at their weaknesses, call themselves "drunks," and exhibit attitudes that are the envy of those around them. Dr. Scott Peck refers to recovering addicts as lucky because "they were kicked into community." Their illness brought them to their knees, forcing them to admit their frailties and to reach out to others for help.

In the beginning, a great many of us believe that what makes us human is our mind. But once we admit our own human weaknesses, we come to believe that what makes us human is our heart. When we are broken, we learn patience and endurance. When we share tears, there is time and space for acceptance.

Life is not the wick or the candle; it is the burning.

WHEN YOU have invested a lot of yourself in something, and then it's no longer there for reasons beyond your control, you are likely to feel a deep sense of loss.

Grief, as a cathartic process, is very useful for moving through these transitions, whether you've lost a job, or a friend, or you've moved. You need to feel the loss fully so that anger and bitterness about wasted time and energy, denial about how much you cared, and other feelings of regret and sorrow can be let go. That requires you to cry them out, to wail and sob until they are no longer an important part of your day—to grieve actively. Alla Bozarth, an Episcopal priest and young widow, writes about surviving her deepest sorrow, concluding a poem with these lines:

> *What I am learning from this*
> *is that I am awakening.*

We must let go of what we've lost and experience all the pain that is the price of renewal.

August 6

EXPOSING AN inner dimension we have hidden away for a lifetime doesn't have to be destructive. If we want to face our fear that our relationship with the people we love would be ruined by full disclosure of our feelings, we may have to reveal how much we sometimes hate them.

That doesn't imply that we want to act out our hate by attacking them physically or verbally, or even by threatening to do so. It is a very different experience for both people when we bracket our awful feelings within the context of our continued caring.

Even after a really awful argument, it's possible to say softly, "I hate how much I hate you at times like these. Because you mean so much to me, I'm scared that now that you know how I feel, you won't ever want to have anything more to do with me."

Instead of one of us having to lose, amazingly we both can win. It's astonishing how two who love each other can hear the caring intended in each other's awful confessions. It's even more astonishing when we can listen and love without trying to change the other.

Real intimacy requires exposing some awful feelings.

WHEN SOMEONE loves you without trying to change you, you gain trust in that other person and confidence in yourself to become who you are.

A relationship like this between lovers creates intimacy. Between parent and child, it is like the dedicated self-discipline of yoga: Maintaining a relationship based on unconditional love is the "yoke that frees."

As Ram Dass has said, "The only thing you have to offer another human being, ever, is your own state of being. . . . You realize that the only thing you have to do for another human being is to keep yourself really straight, and then do whatever it is you do."

Acceptance of the beloved is a gift to both partners.

August 8

IN DEALING with conflicts, the Hasidics said, each of us must begin with ourselves. Rather than simply blaming the other person, we must take on the difficult responsibility of turning our attention to our own part in the problem, with no more than the hope that the other will do the same.

But, the heart-searching involved in conflict or any other of our difficulties is a part of the human struggle that is never solved once and for all by anyone, no matter how holy or how mature one might be.

When the Baal Shem Tov, the first spiritual leader of the Hasidics, was asked how one could tell whether or not a teacher was a real Hasidic rabbi, he suggested that the teacher be asked for advice on how to rid oneself permanently of temptation to evil, how to expel alien thoughts forever. If he offered such advice, he was of no real importance as a teacher. For with the evil urge, "a man must struggle until his last moment, and just that is the service of a man in the world."

We must accept responsibility for ourselves every day for the rest of our lives.

BEING SPECIAL sounds good, but it usually doesn't feel that way. It usually starts with the kind of attention you received in childhood. If your parents pampered and overprotected you, you probably weren't adequately prepared for taking on responsibility. It wasn't that your parents gave you too much but that they also didn't insist on giving you what you needed.

On the other hand, if you were singled out for negative attention, you got an entirely different sense of being special. If your parents weren't adequately prepared to accept you as a person in your own right, they probably protected themselves from taking responsibility for who you were. Your parents may have given a great deal to you, but most often they gave what they needed to give rather than what you needed to receive.

Now you have the chance to take charge of your own feelings. There's still time to give up the old belief of being special ("terminal uniqueness" one AA old-timer called it) and enjoy the comforting reality of being both good and bad like the rest of us.

Accepting that we are ordinary is an unexpected gift.

August 10

THE MORE freely we think, the bolder we can be. When we are bolder than others, we make mistakes that they do not risk making. However, rather than admiring us for our courage, often they simply condemn us for our errors. The criticism of the group may convince us to yield to their pressures, to close our eyes to new possibilities, and to live the safer, surer, more restricted life that the communal rules prescribe. We retain the option of choosing not to give in.

Once you learn to stand alone against a group, typically you find yourself able to face down those less independent people who follow the dictates of the group. This is harder than you think.

In the face of their challenge to your individual position, it's difficult not to be overwhelmed with self-doubt. It's hard to maintain confidence in your personal beliefs when faced with going it alone.

Believing in ourselves can increase our strength.

WATCHING A play, we willingly suspend our disbelief. Until the final curtain, we watch the events on stage as if they are real. Yet, theater itself is a flawed metaphor for life. Watching an evening's performance is clearly a separate experience from life outside the theater. In everyday life, the boundary between the external event and the audience is distinct.

However, the border between personal fantasy and our actual lives is less clear. It is impossible to know for sure when we are seeing the world as it is, and when we are seeing it as we believe it should be. For example, it can be dangerous to believe so completely in people in authority that you don't question whether they are right.

Pursuing final answers to ultimate questions leaves us depressed. Becoming apathetic cynics doesn't feel any better. Knowing that no way of looking at life is any more real than another, we may freely choose those metaphors that make our lives more colorful and our relationships richer. Whether or not God exists, believing in Him (or Her) is an awesome journey. No metaphor is more powerful than this.

Act as if you believe in a higher power.

HUMAN BEINGS cannot become perfect. Evil can be redistributed, but never eliminated. The temptation to cop out is ever present, but maybe all we can hope for is to remain committed to the struggle to do our best.

We all wander in the desert, lost and alone. We suffer, seek some reason, some certainty, some clarity. We want the face of the enemy to be clear at last, and for the good guys to win once and for all. When we forget who we are, we risk becoming a force of evil. We may define ourselves as those who define others, or separate ourselves from others by denying our common humanity.

Our only hope is as a community of exiles, separated from the illusions of childhood, the illusion of the all-good family, and of a secure place in a world that makes sense. It doesn't matter how we came to this point. What matters is that the loss of innocence is permanent. There is no returning. There is only the community of wanderers whose only comfort is to touch the hands of other exiles we meet along the way.

All God's children are lost.

AT TIMES our public image is our only source of self-esteem. No matter how bad we feel privately, we may be able to maintain an image that feels acceptable.

It's no small task to manage the contradiction between a seemingly worthy public self and its often less valued, hidden underside. Qualities we're determined to keep private may seem so appalling to us that they must be ignored, denied, or disowned. Relegating them to the shadows saves us from intolerable feelings of shame and guilt.

Some of these awful secrets are so threatening to our sense of what we're worth that we may hide them from our own awareness as well. Unaware of our own undercover aspects, we may be the only ones we fool.

Worse yet, qualities that we try so hard to hide might actually turn out to be acceptable to others. Some people may love us without demanding that we be something other than what we are.

Self-acceptance is a form of self-improvement.

August 14

SOME PEOPLE try their best to meet other people's expectations. They ask little for themselves and spend most of their time doing for others.

Inevitably, occasions occur when they need something from someone else. Often, they find that they have succeeded so well in presenting an idealized image of self-sufficiency that their friends do not take their temporary neediness seriously.

These chronic do-gooders are astonished and offended that when they finally ask for something, they aren't always seen as automatically entitled to receive it. While living out a contract that by being a good boy (or girl) they will be paid off whenever they request their reward, they have not noticed that no one else has signed the agreement.

Our sacrifices may be worthwhile, but they do not obligate anyone else to do the same for us.

THE WORLD is sometimes kind, but also often harsh. In order to survive, we've had to learn to accommodate other people's expectations.

We contrive a false self as a strategy of compliance, but doing that can get out of hand. After a while our pretense begins to seem real and what we started doing to deceive others fools them less than we fool ourselves.

When our pretending is no longer conscious, the false self turns against us and our true self is betrayed. We project onto other people the unaccepted parts of our selves that we've been trying to keep hidden. We can recognize that we are projecting when we realize that we've overreacted in an encounter with another person, for instance, by getting outraged instead of irritated when someone is thoughtless.

With every projection comes an opportunity for greater self-awareness. Because it's easier at the time, we tend to ignore what we could learn, but in the long run, our short-sighted deceptions make life harder.

We feel better when we are being our natural selves than when we are acting "nice."

TO MAKE radical changes in the way we feel about ourselves, we must reclaim our projections, those shadowy images of our dark side we see reflected on others' faces. However, it isn't easy to restore awareness of disowned parts of the self and admit they are ours.

One lifetime is too short to complete the task. At best, whatever progress we make will be uneven. We'll be required to give up the illusion that our waking rational consciousness is in control and challenged to reconcile our opposites by experiencing multiple realities. We will have to suffer the discomfort of recognizing that all we've banished as not-self is as real a part of us as all the rest.

This does not mean we must decide we're the opposite of who we've always thought we are. Instead, we must accept that all of the contradictory parts of our self are worth something by learning to value every bit of who we are.

We are all filled with contradictions.

WHETHER INTERNAL distress or external circumstances call into question the familiar image of our self, a time of confused identity will follow, that though unsettling, can be useful. Without some temporary disorientation, it isn't possible to make lasting changes in how much or how well we accept ourselves. Losing a job, changing careers, military service, marriage, divorce, becoming a parent, having the youngest child leave home—these are experiences that unsettle and disorient even the most stable personality.

It is the same for all of us. We may submit voluntarily or go kicking and screaming that we cannot stand life as it is. Changes that involve personal growth require that we repeatedly expand our emotional limits and renew our work on the self. In order to do that, as William Butler Yeats said, we must learn that "personality, no matter how habitual, is a constantly renewed choice."

Personal growth is a life's work, not a part-time project.

WHY CAN'T we remember that every time we innocently imagine we can turn a corner without running into the unexpected, we get knocked flat? It's like swimming in the ocean. We seem to enjoy the water so much when it's calm that we turn our backs to the oncoming surf, forgetting the unexpectedly rough wave that hits us from behind, upsetting our balance and washing us into the sand.

Each time we get knocked to the pavement or upended by a wave and rolled in the sand, we eventually pick ourselves up and get on with it. Only then are we rewarded by whatever previously undiscovered treasures occur beyond the unexpected obstacles.

Again and again, we recommit ourselves to thinking about exploring the future. We are certain that next time we will remember to expect the unexpected and to anticipate the surprises.

But we never do.

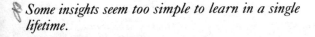 *Some insights seem too simple to learn in a single lifetime.*

MANY OF our unhappy struggles with other people—even those we love—are the outcome of our trying to control each other. Each of us tries to turn the other into what we want him or her to be.

The first step in resolving such struggles is to acknowledge the ways in which our own need to control have contributed to the problem. Then one of us needs to give in. The one who is most aware of his or her part in creating the trouble must be the first one to take responsibility for giving up trying to change the other.

When you are unable to exercise the self-control you intend, try taking charge by indulging your need to be all-powerful. Think about what it would be like to tell the person you're struggling with, "What I really want is to have everything my own way all the time. I want to control you so you will comply with all my desires."

We must be careful not to confuse having our own way with getting what we really want.

August 20

TRYING TO cross the border back into his own country, a young man loses all his identification. As an old story goes, a suspicious policeman waits while the confused and frightened young man frantically searches for his passport. Finally, he finds a candid snapshot and, in desperation, thrusts it at the officer. "See, surely you can see that it's me!" Seeing that it is a photograph of the young tourist's face, the officer lets him go with an apology: "After all, how could *you* be wrong about who you are?"

Imagine being mistaken about who you think you are. That's one of the few things in life you don't have to worry about. Or is it? What about those embarrassing moments when something you did unintentionally revealed a discrepancy between your image of yourself and that seemingly less acceptable person you sometimes turn out to be. Such disruptions make us feel self-conscious. Then we realize just how vulnerable we can feel when confronted with the deceptively simple question, "Who am I?"

The false images we create to conceal our real selves from others may fool us as well.

SENTIMENTALITY HAS been said to involve our bringing more soft feelings to the world than God did when He created it. This is not simply a matter of taste. Often people who are sentimental attend to the sweet side of life while ignoring the brutal aspect, either discounting or denying reality. They see the blossoms, but not the thorns.

Life can be experienced as lovely, but its horror has to be acknowledged as well. Steinbeck wrote, "If you want to see life in the raw, look into a tidal pool." Much of nature is made up of prey and predators.

Ironically, sentimentalists can be brutal when anyone threatens to shatter their illusions. As William Inge wrote, "Experience proves that none is so cruel as the disillusioned sentimentalist."

Waiting for life to be lovely before you start to live is like waiting for the river to run out before you cross.

August 22

WE HAVE idealized images of ourselves. Not only do we picture ourselves in the roles that we have assumed but we also expect others to react to us as if we were what we say we are.

Among the many stereotyped postures people assume are those of the regular guy or the maverick, the femme fatale or the stud, the proper lady or the gentleman, the devotee to social causes or the high-tech, acquiring yuppie. We dress in accordance with our chosen images, and assume the mannerisms and jargon that fit the models.

We are surprised and disappointed when other people see through our stylized postures, and judge us by how we actually live our lives rather than by the words and appearance that are the hype of our public relations.

It does no good to talk the talk if you can't walk the walk.

SOME PEOPLE seem to believe that they make something special of themselves by concentrating on matters so esoteric that very few others find what they have to say of interest. They pride themselves on not seeing popular movies, only foreign films, not reading best-selling books, only avant-garde fiction, and doing nothing so plebeian as watching television. They see themselves as too creative to speak the way other people do or to attend to everyday matters with which we all have to deal.

Hoping to be celebrated as original thinkers, frequently these self-appointed specialists end up as oddballs who bore audiences with their pedantry. Their dedication to humankind is belied by their insensitivity to the needs of individual people in their lives. They deceive themselves by imagining that their own greatness is implied in their unusual special interests.

Ironically, as Elbert Hubbard wrote, "Little minds are interested in the extraordinary; great minds in the commonplace."

Ordinary human beings are interesting, just as they are.

COUPLES ARE often made up of pairs of opposites in their way of experiencing the world. Thinking types often marry feeling types and intuitive people frequently choose action-oriented partners. These differences in outlook can offer both a complementary balance in a couple and they can become the underlying issue in the worst of their chronic arguments.

The differences between the two types may be inborn differences in temperament. But if you find that you are at one or the other extreme of the spectrum, you do have the option of trying to develop its counterpart by attending carefully to whatever is going on in the function you are less likely to use naturally.

You need to go against your grain: Thinkers need to pay more attention to what goes on in their hearts, just as feelers must try to think things out before saying something to their partners. The intuitive people must attend to the facts and the sensation types need to dwell on the implications of their actions.

Whether or not we should do what comes naturally may depend on the situation.

ANYONE WHO hasn't developed a self that is truly his or her own lives a life that is a shallow showpiece. The little nourishment they get is restricted to the approval they receive in return for pleasing others. It's a little like making a meal for friends while you yourself have to settle for licking the serving spoon.

Doing for others can be a genuine source of happiness in and of itself, but not without taking care of yourself as well. In the same way, doing as you please may allow you a joyous sense of freedom, but it's unsatisfying if ignoring the needs of others results in the emptiness of isolation.

Where do we draw the line? How can we strike a balance? All we can do is take our best shot and try to learn from our mistakes.

There are no hard and fast rules for living with others.

WHEN SOMEONE disagrees with us, even when we have asked for an honest opinion, it often sets off an alarm within us, a kind of call to battle to defend our position, to fortify our defenses. Somehow our intelligence and even self-worth feel called into question.

Our temptation is to put down the threat by restricting others' freedom of expression. We may try this overtly, by discounting them by saying, "No one in their right mind would believe that!" Or we may covertly try to retaliate, perhaps giving them the cold shoulder, making snide remarks, and so on.

We may be successful in putting down our opposition, but if we do so, the next victim of censorship will probably turn out to be us. When Voltaire said, "I do not agree with a word you have said, but would fight to the death for your right to say it," he was protecting his own freedom as well.

When we cost others their freedom, we risk being caged ourselves.

AS WE review our lives, we become aware of the many mistakes we have made—things we would do differently, if given a second chance. Our regrets can be useful reminders of how to do better the next time a similar situation arises. But it is one thing to learn from past mistakes and another to make ourselves miserable about them.

We must learn to forgive ourselves for past errors that we made because we were unprepared, or unaware of the consequences, or ignorant of better options that might have been chosen.

Regret can be instructive, but remorse is a waste of time.

August 28

SOME PEOPLE are uncomfortable verbally expressing their appreciation and affection simply and directly to the person they care about. Instead, they either assume that the other person should know how they feel, or they tell a third party how wonderful it is to have their beloved in their lives, and hope that the message will get back to them.

Other examples of misguided messages can be seen when parents boast to friends about how proud they are of their children, but never tell the children directly how pleased they are. Or when supervisors find it easier to tell employees that they should be doing as well as some others without ever extending the accolade to the ones who earned it.

You can't send a kiss by messenger.

THOMAS WOLFE wrote of war making the world safe for hypocrisy. War heightens our sense of the artificial distinction between the good guys and the bad guys. In patriotic frenzy, we lose sight of the fact that the enemy is made up of other human beings with whom we disagree. We forget that this decade's foe may be the next one's friend.

In passionate personal arguments, we sometimes experience the same sort of fantasied transformations. We can share a friendship for years, but in the midst of a rage-filled conflict, it's easy to lose sight of all the good feelings we've had and might yet have again with this momentary opponent who has now become a monster in our own angelic eyes.

A weapon may have an innocent victim at each end.

THE MOST important person in each of our lives is ourself. Truly loving someone else means that we are sometimes willing to reset our priorities by putting their happiness ahead of our own. If this is done out of loving devotion, it makes us happy as well, but our pleasure is secondary to the joy of the beloved.

But love is tricky terrain. If what we give our loved one is offered as a sacrifice, then it is not a gift of devotion but an act of martyrdom. We do it to enhance our own image of ourselves, or in exchange for anticipated appreciation.

There is a parallel in helping a stranger. If we do so out of a need to be nice, rather than as an act of compassion, we are confusing manners with morals. If it doesn't come from the heart, the stranger may be grateful, but for us it will still feel like a sin of pride.

It's easy to confuse being loving with acting out of duty or ego.

THE URGE to commit evil exists within all of us, but even that is a part of us, a life force to be reclaimed and transformed, rather than rejected. When we can get in touch with and accept every part of ourselves, we won't continually have to be at war within ourselves.

If a thief comes in the night and we cry out and scare him off, nothing is accomplished beyond the moment, and we must remain in fear. But if we do not alarm the thief, yet let him draw near enough so that we can get hold of him and bind him, then we have a chance of reforming him.

In the same way, our own stubbornness can be transformed into determination, and our struggles with each other can dissolve into intimacy. However, each of us must confront ourselves in order to accomplish these transformations, this turning of the self.

We must come to own the evil within us.

September 1

WE WASTE too much time immersed in anxiety about whether we are good or bad. We'd be better off expending our energy on simply taking care of all that needs doing. A tale is told of a young Buddhist monk who worried a lot. While walking through the forest to return to his monastery, he came upon an old Zen master. Delighted to have found an audience for his obsessions, he tried to strike up a conversation with the seemingly carefree older man.

The young monk talked a great deal, mostly about himself. The old man listened and smiled, but didn't seem to have much to say. Then the young man declared, "I became a monk to attain spiritual enlightenment. For a long while, I was afraid I would never attain a saintly attitude, but my years of service have paid off and now I have become quite humble."

"How about you?" he asked the old man. "Are you humble?"

After a few minutes, the master replied, "I don't really know. I've never thought much about it."

In our right pocket we need to keep one reminder: "For my sake God created the universe," and in our left pocket another: "I am dust and ashes."

ONE WOMAN said, "I've put myself in the hands of many masters, but none really knew the true meaning of life. I tried everything they said, but nothing helped for long. I am still unhappy." She had actively transferred responsibility for management of her life from one professional caretaker to another, firing the most recent helper to go off in search of someone else with better magic. Ever hopeful, she went on being unhappy and suffering repeated disappointments.

Finally, she met someone who knew a few answers and a few tricks, but who said he wouldn't help her. She pleaded on many occasions, but to no avail. "You're not giving me the answers again today!" she would exclaim. "Why won't you tell me what to do? You act like what I do with my life is all up to me!" She paused, hardly believing what she had just said.

"Do you mean to tell me that this is all there is to it? I spend all these years trying to find someone to look after me and then end up giving myself the answer— that I have to run my own life?"

We're the only ones who can find our answers.

September 3

"WE MUST first change into nothing if we want to change from one reality to another. To become a new creature, we must cease to be the creature that we are," wrote Dr. Maurice Friedman in *A Dialogue with Hasidic Tales*. He then repeated words from the Hasidic tradition:

The kernel which is sown in earth must fall to pieces so that the ear of grain can sprout from it. Strength cannot be resurrected until it has dwelt in deep secrecy. To doff a shape, to don a shape—this is done in the instant of pure nothingness . . . . On the day of destruction, power lies at the bottom of the depths and grows.

Just as the phoenix rises again out of the ashes, when we are at our worst, we discover how to recover ourselves. When we are in the deepest despair, we fall to the ground. From there we can look up and see the light.

Out of the silence comes the song.

SOME MORNINGS, we wake up feeling that it's a glorious day to be alive. Others, we awaken depressed that we have yet another day to live through.

Depending on our mood, we may view death as either too distant or too near at hand. There is little we can do that may delay death other than attempt to keep fit and play it safe. Only suicide can assuredly hasten its coming. Both strategies have been known to fail.

The crucial decision we might make is to live each day as if it were our last. If we have lived the previous day as well and as fully as we might, then when we awaken the next morning, we can arise in the Native American tradition of opening our eyes wide with the wonder of life, at the same time saying simply, "Today would be a good day to die!"

The inevitability of death is easier to accept after a life well lived.

September 5

DO WE need people or don't we? This question has caused much confusion for many people, as each searches for love and for meaning. The answer is yes. Yes, we do need other people—and yes, we don't.

We need love and we need to be loved. We have family; we make friends; we belong to a community. We need some other people *to be with us*, as a life-affirming part of our lives.

But we don't need those other people *to be us*, for then we aren't. In other words, we cannot look to others to fill the needs that only we can fill for ourselves. If we depend on them to be responsible for what they cannot do, the natural consequence will be failure to have our hopes fulfilled. No one can make us feel good about ourselves. No one can take away our shame. No one can give us peace or make us happy.

If you are willing to accept just how scared and helpless you sometimes feel, you'll spend less of your life fighting off depression and anxiety, feeling like a victim, and denying your own adequacy. You may also find some intimate companions along the way.

Live well and others may join you.

IT'S IMPORTANT to know when you're angry and at whom. This gives you the option of choosing whether or not to express your irritation openly. In a political situation (such as dealing with your boss or a policeman), where the consequences of open expression of anger seem too costly, you may decide to keep your mouth shut. But you need not feel stuck with your unspoken resentment. Instead, you can tell someone you trust about how frustrating it feels to be mistreated by people too dangerous to take on by fighting back directly.

In personal relationships, it will serve you better not to let irritation accumulate. In the long run, your suppressed feelings will make themselves felt by your withdrawal from someone you care about or by some later unintended, exaggerated outburst. Even with people who matter personally, you don't always need to counterattack what you experience as abuse. Instead, you can talk with them about how awful it feels to be angry with someone you love.

At times building walls between people is necessary, but building bridges feels better.

September 7

WE ALL have thoughts and experience feelings that we've been taught are not on the approved list. In the Bible the list appears as the Ten Commandments. These temptations must be universal, or it wouldn't have been necessary to elevate these cautions to rules laid down by God.

But the inner life of our imaginations is not only private territory—it is also God-given. When we allow ourselves to envision the unthinkable and to say the unspeakable, we are only thinking and saying what most people keep to themselves.

We solitary pilgrims pursue a spiral path from the outer edge of our imagination to the interior of our soul.

REACHING OUT to make other people's lives more pleasant can bring us happiness as well. But it is not enough for those of us who are devoting ourselves to saintly self-sacrifice and service as a way of trying to overcome the belief that we are undeserving. It's a bit like baking cakes for everyone else and limiting celebration of your own birthdays to licking off the icing that gets smeared on your fingers.

There is a balance point we each must find that best serves how we want to live—somewhere along the continuum of taking care of other people and taking care of ourselves. Often, it's a difficult judgment call. Some of us do too much for others and not enough for ourselves, while some others do the opposite. It is helpful to understand which direction we usually lean toward. Once our inclinations become clear, we can deal with uncertain situations by trying to err in the opposite direction.

Learn to make mistakes that are the opposite of your usual errors.

TOO OFTEN good deeds go unrewarded, while evil goes unpunished. If we don't believe in an afterlife, how are we to make our way through the seemingly arbitrary disorder of the unfairness we so often encounter?

Camus strove "to be a just man in an unjust world." The reward for undertaking this contradiction lies in the input we make, rather than in the outcome of our lives. His choice was to "neither victim nor executioner be." In other words, it's okay to take care of ourselves, but not at the expense of others.

We may never know a world devoid of poverty and oppression, but we must continue to try to bring it about nonetheless. Like the Man of La Mancha, "We must live the impossible dream."

We give our lives meaning and worth by trying to do the right thing.

SOME PEOPLE feel so awful if they are single that they mate carelessly out of a desperate wish to avoid being alone. Carl Whitaker warns, "If you really want to experience loneliness, get married." The most painful form of loneliness is feeling alone while in the company of an emotionally inaccessible partner.

Some people have been so badly disappointed by past romances that they vow never to love again. In self-protective isolation, they even avoid making close friends and settle for having acquaintances with whom they share shallow alliances set up to have company in activities of mutual interest.

Keeping busy becomes a substitute for risking the dangers of loving once again. It passes the time, but the time will pass in any case. While it passes, why not invest yourself in closer, more enriching relationships? You may well get hurt again, but as W. H. Auden wrote, "We must love one another, or die."

Without love, what kind of life do we have?

OFTEN WE treat with disdain what others do well that we cannot. We mask our envy with contempt. For example, take two female college students: one an openly studious young woman who is ill at ease with displaying her femininity; the other an academic underachiever who is popular with many of the young men she meets. Each is potentially bright and attractive, but the male-shy, overachiever sees the popular poor student as a hot-blooded airhead and, in return, is seen herself as a frigid bookworm.

As a second example, consider two male college students: One derides the other as unstable or unreliable because he goes to extremes to display his idiosyncrasies, while the eccentric dismisses the other as lacking in imagination and daring because he tries to be just one of the regular guys.

What sets these pairs at odds with each other is exactly those attributes that one has and the other could use. If they could drop their defensive disdain and openly express the admiration implicit in their envy, each could instruct and comfort the other. The secrets they could share might help make each of them a more complete human being.

Caricature must not be confused with character.

IT CAN be easier to spend time with people who are a little crazy but who admit they're peculiar than with those who insist that they are sane and that the rest of us are the ones with problems.

The same is true with people who keep their opinions in perspective and those who don't. A person whose outlook seems mistaken to us can sometimes be more fun to be with than someone who shares our sense of right and wrong. As Will Rogers said, "Everybody is ignorant, only on different subjects."

When we move to music others can't hear, they may see us as mad dancers.

SOME PEOPLE enter relationships with the hope that someday they'll be happy with the person they've chosen because their partner will change to become more of who they want them to be. These "promising" dreams of future happiness almost always turn out to be nightmares.

People do change, but only if they themselves are ready to do so, and often more easily with the support of someone who already accepts them. If, at the outset of our coming together, we are already satisfied with each other, we have the best chance that our relationship can become even better.

Rather than trying to change one another, we need to spend enough time together to get to know one another as well as we can.

If you want to work on improving someone, try working on yourself.

THE TEMPTATION to avoid emotional pain is easy to understand, but if we put off confronting acute anguish, often our procrastination costs us much more than we might otherwise have had to pay. It's like buying assurance on an installment plan. We may get away with not having to make an initial down payment, but the interest can be exorbitant and the periodic outlays seem to go on forever.

For example, if we are abused by those who matter to us, it's difficult to give up hope that eventually they will treat us well. We insist that someday they will see what they're doing wrong or that we can find a way to fix whatever we imagine we've done to merit being treated badly. Because we cannot imagine ever getting over the acute grief we would have to endure to escape our daily pain, some of us remain in the victim position for a lifetime. Refusing to mourn, instead we go on complaining without changing anything.

Giving up on an abusive relationship takes courage. Support from others helps, but not enough to spare us the deep disappointment and grief we must endure. It remains our own personal responsibility to decide to risk being alone. But being alone is not the same as being lonely. At least we have ourselves and the option of finding others to love who will treat us better. We can make the difficult choice or go on fussing and hoping for the rest of our lives.

Some relationships are not worth trying to repair.

MANY PEOPLE assume that, beneath the surface, those who deviate from the norm are all basically "just like the rest of us." Societal standards are taken to be God-given models that everyone wants to live up to. Those who don't have simply failed to attain them.

It is difficult to accept that deviance can be an inherent peculiarity of some people, a difference that they do not necessarily wish to correct. Some mental health professionals may call such people "dysfunctional," but it's a mistake to assume that everyone wants to be "normal" without first asking them who they want to be or how they want to live.

We assume, for instance, that inside every fat person is a thin person trying to get out, but Kingsley Amis writes that "Outside every fat man, there is an even fatter man trying to close in."

How wonderful it is that there are so many ways we differ from one another.

LISTENING CAREFULLY allows us to hear what is not being said. Frequently, we avoid stating our feelings directly for fear we'll get hurt or hurt someone else, so our most pressing message is obscured or hidden completely.

For instance, when you interrupt a statement to take another tack, it often indicates a deliberate decision to hide an unacceptable feeling.

If you offer a gratuitous denial such as saying, "I'm not angry," when no one asked if you were, some part of you is mad and another part is suppressing open expression of the feeling.

"I don't *really* feel upset," indicates that there are ways in which you really do.

Even though we try to disguise the seemingly unacceptable part of our message, our intent is either known or felt. So is another disconcerting message—that we've tried, and failed, to obscure the fact that we have a hidden agenda.

Gratuitous denials require our attention.

BERTRAND RUSSELL wrote, "Of all forms of caution, caution in love is perhaps most fatal to true happiness."

No one wants to suffer a broken heart. To protect our most vulnerable feelings, some of us approach the encompassing circle of love gingerly, as if with one foot in and the other out. We may be willing to sort of care for someone, but only if we know we can get over it, sometimes simply by meeting another who seems more appealing.

If we mistake surrender for defeat, then commitment and devotion feel more like being caged than like coming home. To guard ourselves from the pain of abandonment or betrayal, we may refuse to put our hearts in the hands of another. But when we avoid accepting anyone as our beloved, we sacrifice softness and warmth that cannot come from loving cautiously.

Broken hearts mend, but the emptiness of untested love leaves a hole in the soul that may never be filled.

CARING ABOUT others from the abundance of a full heart can be a wonderful offering to others. But, if self-sacrifice is a way of filling an empty place in the giver, often the result is a kind of martyrdom. The self-serving martyr may ask more in return than the other person receives.

When giving comes with strings attached, the receiver isn't necessarily obligated to the giver and need not be burdened by the guilt that the giver is covertly contracting for. Instead, we can beware of martyrs bearing gifts and to tell them, "Do me a favor: Don't do me any favors!"

Or if we feel entitled to being treated well and also free from unwarranted obligation, we can simply say, "Thanks a lot," take the money, and run.

A gift is not a loan that requires repayment.

September 19

SOME PEOPLE complain that they don't have a chance to confront people who mistreat them, pleading they didn't know how they felt until it was too late to do anything about it. Using this lack of awareness in the moment of conflict as an excuse means the same submissive behavior is sure to continue.

There is another option. It's often possible to write or call the offending person as soon as we recognize that we've been abused. It's also possible to take the matter up the next time we meet. This may seem like a way of making unnecessary trouble, but in the long run, it amounts to accepting responsibility for one deliberate piece of unpleasantness, rather than passively encouraging unintended repeated occasions of conflict.

When we give up using our slow uptake as an excuse, gradually the gap will close between the time we are mistreated and the moment we recognize how upset we are. And unless we are willing to deliberately confront those who mistreat us, helplessness and resentment build up that will ruin the relationship.

It pays to go back and clean up whatever messes we've overlooked.

WHEN WE don't feel entitled to having our wishes fulfilled, paradoxically, we may become demandingly dependent. For example, a friend asks what movie we'd like to go to see together. We answer, "Whatever you want to see will be fine with me." The other person mentions two nearby film showings and expresses a preference. It's not the one we would have chosen, but our muted complaint is expressed only in our unenthusiastic tone.

Our friend hears what we are pretending not to communicate and suggests that instead we attend the other film. Instead of graciously accepting the accommodation to our unclearly stated wishes, we ask again and again, "Are you sure that's all right with you?" If we continue these pesky demands for reassurance, then the next time we go out our friend may well not bother to feed our insatiable hunger for being told that it's all right for us to get what we want.

If there's something you want, ask for it; you'll have a better chance of getting it.

PEOPLE WHO want to establish long-term, intimate relationships must be ready to make commitments. No matter how wonderful it feels when we first fall in love, we can be certain that there will be some hard times ahead. The golden glow of idealization will flicker from time to time. Eventually it will fade away.

Most romantic relationships begin with idyllic passion, but it takes more than this to maintain whatever remains worthwhile. Inevitably, we begin to see each other's wrinkles and warts as well. Still, the promise of "for better or for worse, till death do us part" poses its own sorts of problems. Devotion is crucial to enduring the ordeals of discord, yet knowing that you are staying together by choice helps to make hard times easier to bear. The unbearable feeling of being helplessly trapped makes it more difficult for couples to be patient enough to work through their conflicts.

When the going gets tough in a relationship we must learn to work together.

CYNICS AND sentimentalists are at opposite ends of the attitude spectrum. If sentimentalists optimistically insist on looking at the bright side, cynics always expect the worst. They build their pessimistic lives on doubt, distrust, and disbelief.

Either side has its own shadow. A sentimentalist whose naive hopefulness is threatened can be unexpectedly brutal. This is matched by the doubting Thomas whose shadow side can surface as an unexpected capacity for devotion when converted to a religious dogma.

To live to the full, we must be both tender and tough, ready to accept life for both its beauty and its brutality.

September 23

WHEN EVERYTHING we think and feel and do seems completely clear and right, we are really in big trouble. We may have bought into a cultlike system of beliefs that assures us that life can be lived in the absence of contradictions. If so, the cure can be worse than the disease.

Another sort of reassuring trap, though this one is not usually supported by others, is having an inflated sense of confidence. This has to be kept in place by pride and rigidity in order to protect us from the threatening awareness of just how little we know for sure.

Whatever way we became so sure of everything we believe, the best antidote is confusion and uncertainty. Without this "holy insecurity," our beliefs go untested, and we are unable to learn anything new. Just as religious doubts can strengthen faith in God, self-doubt can clarify our outlook and encourage more realistic confidence in our self.

Confusion can be just what we need to help clarify our thinking.

WE CANNOT make ourselves happy simply by deciding that we are going to "party" and have fun. But some of us miss out on many of the opportunities for joy that occur in our lives.

We can become so preoccupied with regrets about the past and worries about the future that we either overlook the pleasures available in the present, or we feel too gloomy and sorry for ourselves to enjoy seizing whatever each new moment affords.

Our concern for what we don't have also makes it difficult to share the happiness in other people's lives. Self-pity and envy are poor substitutes for enjoying whatever is sweet in a life that is not all we wish it to be.

Take joy wherever you find it.

September 25

THE SPIRIT and the soul are not the same. Metaphorically, we think of our spirit as trying to ascend toward angelic perfection—all light and no heat. On the other hand, our soul goes through a spiraling descent toward the depths of all that is human.

Spiritual seeking is an attempt to transcend frailty; it is a cleansing accomplishment. Unfortunately, it is also accompanied by an evangelical insistence on saving all the other people who have not yet risen to as high a spiritual plane as we imagine we have reached.

Soul searching is more like giving in to acceptance of our impurities and affirming that it's okay that we're not all we've been taught to expect ourselves to be. It's less a triumph of overcoming than a surrender to the way we are. Earnest soul searchers don't try to convert other people. They know that everyone already has everything that is needed and hope they are able to enjoy the fun of how funky we all are. Too often self-righteous seekers try to rise on the shoulders of sinners below.

To rise up to a higher plane, we must begin by heading down and into ourselves.

SOME OF us are disdainful and suspicious whenever anyone acts kindly toward us. We wonder what they're up to or what they're after. It's difficult to imagine there is no ulterior motive masked by their apparent generosity. As a result, we withdraw in ways that leave them feeling rejected. Or we may meet them with wariness that they find critical and off-putting. When they back away from us as a result, we experience their defensive reaction as confirmation that our original suspicions were correct.

Some of us acquired this distrust from dealing with repeated experiences of unexpected betrayal early in our lives. At the time, being suspicious was a sensible reaction, but our residual distrust often is no longer needed.

The only cure for our paranoia is grief. We need to reexperience the anguish of having trusted and been betrayed, to feel the depth of our disappointment, and to mourn our losses. Eventually we'll be willing to trust once more. Certainly we risk being hurt again, but if we don't, we give up hope of ever getting what some other people might be happy to give us.

Sometimes it's better to be sorry than safe.

September 27

IT'S IMPORTANT for us to learn what we might say or do that is likely to hurt someone's feelings. We need to be especially attentive to the heightened vulnerability of members of oppressed groups. Also, whenever possible, we need to keep in mind the idiosyncratic sore spots of anyone we're dealing with.

Having this information is necessary, but not sufficient. If we want to avoid hurting someone's feelings without intending to do them harm, we then must willingly attend carefully to what we understand about whatever might feel abrasive to their vulnerability.

Once we understand and attend to how to avoid hurting another person accidentally, we also accrue the fringe benefit of having a more relaxed relationship with that person.

Try not to hurt anyone unless you really mean to.

NO MATTER how powerful we are, or imagine ourselves to be, some people are stronger. However powerless we may feel, others are weaker. But like so many human assets, power can be both a crown and a cross. The advantages of having power are numerous, but they may inflate our sense of self-importance and encourage us to exploit other people.

The old adage that "power corrupts" is accurate, but as Adlai Stevenson said, "the absence of power also corrupts."

If we want personal freedom, we must learn to temper appreciation for power when we have it with respect for others when they don't. We must take responsibility for both our power and our helplessness. It sounds simple, but it isn't easy.

Although it makes sense to seek power when we feel helpless, we must take responsibility for how we use whatever power we may attain.

MANY PEOPLE have been taught that anger is bad. Some have been raised to believe that even feeling angry is wrong, and that expressing it openly is far worse. Despite these expectations, we find ourselves enraged at times.

When we were very young children, we already had much of what we seek on our adult spiritual quests. We lived in the here and now, and acted with the Zen spontaneity of "first thought, best thought." When we were angry or hurting, we cried out, and as soon as our frustrations were eased, we returned to seizing the joy of the moment.

Now as adults, we repeatedly hold back our anger and try to ignore our resentment, but then our feelings burst out unexpectedly. We express our hostility at inappropriate times, directed toward people who don't deserve it, in ways that are exaggerated by the buildup that accrues because of our denial. We're better off being aware of our anger as it occurs than denying we feel resentful and ending up unpredictably irritable.

Denial increases the dangers of what we fear.

SOME PEOPLE assume postures so heroic that no one can imagine that, at times, they need help. Others seem so eccentric that cries for help go unrecognized and misunderstood. As the English poet, Stevie Smith, wrote of herself,

> *I was much too far out all my life,*
> *And not waving but drowning.*

If we want to avoid going under when help is available, we must learn to find ways of communicating our helplessness and distress—ways that others can respond to and understand.

Some of us "would rather die" than willingly expose our frailties. Unfortunately, we may get our wish. It may be true that "pride goeth before a fall," but it is also true that humility is needed if we are to get someone to come to help us up.

When we lose ourselves to experiencing the moment, we leave our development to the Higher Power within us.

4

WHERE DO I GO FROM HERE?

We make the path by walking.
—ROBERT BLY

My pilgrimage . . . will not end so long as I live. And now I know that I shall live, for as long as life is given to me. And should my body be battered even more, then I will live as I can, enjoying what I might . . . and being what I may to the people I love.
—SHELDON KOPP

October 1

"WHEN ONE has organized his life around something and then it's lost, it is devastating. . . . You wonder, 'What am I going to do now? How can I bear to live?'" These are questions posed by Arnold Beisser, a physician paralyzed by polio early in his career. After more than thirty years of a full though physically limited life, Dr. Beisser described his thoughts in *Flying Without Wings*:

> The "Why me?" question and the anger are all parts of the bereavement process. . . . But I realized that digging in to try to avoid dying, being preoccupied with that, keeps one from living life.
>
> Life experiences are always transitory and that includes the worst ones as well as the good ones. Things look pretty black at night, then in the morning they look brighter. . . . Depression is the great deceiver.

It's pointless to go on asking, "Why me?" The only worthwhile question is, "Where do I go from here?"

PEOPLE WHO are only able to see their own realities and seem to live them without question are very apt to discredit our ways of experiencing things. But we must be free from letting anyone else define how we feel.

Our best protection against the half-life of seeing things through others' eyes is the development of an imagination in which all things are possible. To do this, it is necessary to give up the security of a single known reality. A song by Kris Kristofferson points out that realities are no more than possibilities, because "truth is the perfect disguise."

Other people may matter to us in their own way, but no one else can define the meaning of our lives for us.

We each have our own fictions that we call "reality."

October 3

WHEN OUR loved ones show appreciation for something we do, we feel good about ourselves, as well as about whatever we did. Unfortunately, the approval of other people is an undependable source of self-esteem. When they don't appreciate what we do, we tend to feel bad, taking their disapproval to mean there must be something wrong with us, instead of with what we've done.

Fortunately, there are measures of our worth that are more reliable than the approval of others. In place of depending on the love of others to make us feel worthwhile, we can substitute the joyful feeling that comes from loving them. When we become attentive to how good it feels to be with those we love (or even simply remembering what it's like to be with them), we can claim wonderful feelings that are entirely in our hands.

Measuring our worth by how much we are loved by others may make us feel special at times, but the price we pay is the sense of insignificance we suffer when that confirmation is unavailable. The exaltation we feel when we allow someone else to mean a great deal to us is an affirmation that can be counted on even at times when they don't seem to be loving us back.

Our happiness depends more on our own capacity for loving than on our being loved by others.

THOSE WHO have suffered oppression by other, stronger groups, and those who have been hit by a debilitating blow of fate are truly victims. Yet, according to social commentator Joseph Epstein, there's a disturbing new twist today: Too often people merely declare themselves victims, then claim they are powerless and exploited.

Unfortunately, the new victims must find enemies to blame. Also, in order to perpetuate the supposed oppressors' enemy status, victims have to maintain their anger, indulging in what Epstein calls "the contemporary joys of victimhood—the assumption of moral superiority, the spread of guilt, the shifting of responsibility for one's own destiny."

It is ironic that some self-styled victims—those who have had good enough luck not to be physically or politically disadvantaged and good enough love not to have permanent emotional damage—have chosen to restrict themselves from freedom that is theirs for the taking.

Victims are entitled to our compassion, but not if they have chosen their own misfortune.

October 5

AS VERY small children, most of us saw our world as a safe, familiar, well-ordered place. If we were good, we were rewarded. If we were sick, we were tended with care. But, too soon, we grew older and began to find life filled with danger, contradiction, and unfairness. Too often, we found ourselves disappointed and our beliefs in people and systems betrayed.

Everyone has experienced the yearning to return to a time and a place where we felt so loved and well taken care of that it was safe to be completely trusting. Even those who've never had such a haven may yearn for it.

Clinging to outgrown innocence, we are needlessly disappointed again and again, while we miss out on what we may have if we accept the fact that we have to take care of ourselves. Partial freedom and limited happiness are all that are available, and if we want to have at least that much, we'll have to accept those conditions.

We must learn to take care of ourselves every day for the rest of our lives.

WHEN LIFE deals with us in a way we consider unfair, we dream of righteous vengeance and wait for the time when we will be able to conquer all evil and, better yet, to be recognized and appreciated at last. Along with this dream, we also imagine that once we've been so heroic, we can expect to live happily ever after.

These oversimplified notions imply an order to life that doesn't exist. Clinging to this version of perfection robs us of the power to take on that lifelong adult struggle between our ideals and the imperfect situations with which we all must contend.

Life offers no guarantee that we will not fall on hard times again. Accepting painful experiences openly and honestly eliminates the needless suffering that happens when, believing we're special and that the world is fair and just, our bubble bursts one more time.

We must try to live a just life in an unjust world.

October 7

THERE'S NO way in this life to be certain that what you're doing is right. You have to figure things out as best as you can, know what you feel, say what you mean, and do what you say. You have to risk being the fool (again), hope what you do works, and forgive yourself if it doesn't.

Since nobody knows for sure what is right and no one has a monopoly on truth, we should each take a look at the way we see authority, especially in the people we look to for answers. It may be useful to have someone in charge, but to make a leader seem to be more than an ordinary human being makes less of us as followers.

Because of human dependency or transference reactions, we will all be tempted again and again to cast the authority into the hero role. But when we see someone in such a position as bigger, stronger, wiser, or more reliable than we are, a piece of our own worth may be sacrificed to his image.

Not knowing for sure what's right or wrong, all you can do is take your best shot.

THOUGH CERTAIN kinds of pretending may lead to neurotic character styles, pretending is by no means destructive in and of itself. Creative pretending in the form of fantasy and daydreaming gives us pleasure, excitement, relief, and even hope. And pretending can provide a way of filling personal needs at times and in places where we would otherwise have to do without. Each culture provides sanctioned ways of pretending that take people beyond the frustrations of everyday life—experiences such as the enthrallment of the theater and the grandeur of ceremony.

Pretending also mines the mother lode of our imaginations. In fantasy we may find inspiration for new ways to live. In reflection we can even work through practical plans, avoiding much wasted trial-and-error bungling. In daydreaming we may visualize future actions, rehearsing so that we can approach the situations with less fear and more grace.

Without quite knowing what we're after, we must search our souls and listen to our hearts.

October 9

HOW IS a person ever to know what is real and freely chosen in the here and now? Very often the option we choose seems so right, so real, so reasonable, yet we eventually realize that we actually had no choice, because our behavior was influenced in ways we are not prepared to expect by unrecognized experiences in our past.

Sorting out when our choices are essentially free and not unduly influenced by past experiences is often difficult. For some people, checking on what others think is a help. But for the rest of us, without the possibility of being certain, we must learn to do the best we can and to find that sufficient.

We can either tolerate uncertainty or make up the answers.

LIFE IS sometimes painful, often unfair, perhaps always absurd, but it is not tragic. The word *tragedy* implies that there's a moral significance to a disastrous ending and that the victim has somehow caused his or her own downfall. The words *tragedy* and *tragic* are used so often and so loosely that they seem to describe what are really universal human experiences of undeserved calamity.

Someone dies young; an adult is killed while trying to rescue a trapped child; innocent bystanders are killed at the scene of a crime. We shake our heads sadly and declare, "What a tragedy!"

If we view all life and death as tragic, then we believe ourselves to be victims doomed to meet unhappy endings as a result of our own flaws. This may be what happens in the end, but life is not a play and a tragic conclusion is not inevitable. If we want to live life, rather than just play at it, we must choose our own roles and avoid casting ourselves in a tragedy.

When we stop exaggerating the importance of our problems, we'll be left with no more than an ordinary share of unhappiness.

October 11

WHEN PEOPLE feel compelled to seek someone who *really* loves them, it's usually because, in the first few years of life, they had a brief experience of continuous good mothering (from either parent), but at some point the mothering parent lost interest, turned to another child, or simply rejected them.

The arbitrariness of this loss is too painful a concept for helpless children to bear. Rather than accept that their being given up was nothing personal, the children begin to feel that it must be their own fault. They may spend a lifetime blaming themselves, trying to find out what is wrong with them, trying to be the sort of person who will be *really* loved once more.

These people have to go through a great deal of grieving and pain before they can accept that they were ever really loved or that they were not the cause of the loss. Whatever the reason our parents gave up loving us, the betrayal experience must be dealt with—and then we must get on with it.

We don't have the power to make someone love us.

THE WAY we think and talk about problems reflects not only how we feel but also influences what we will do to solve them. If, for example, we believe that we can't stand the pressures of work and family obligations anymore, we may talk ourselves into feeling desperate enough to do anything to get out. No matter how shortsighted or irresponsible our actions might be, at that moment, we are choosing to disregard the fact that the consequences of getting out will only create more pain.

Instead of adding to our misery, another option is to recognize that no matter how dreadful our distress is, we *can* stand it—we know that because we already have stood it. Once we understand that our apparent need to escape is simply a wish for relief, we are free to choose solutions that won't create new problems. Sometimes the best idea is simply to wait problems out. In the meantime, it helps to have someone around who knows what we're going through, and who cares enough to support us without making things worse.

After all, it's only pain. Although it may seem unbearable, it will pass.

EVEN THOUGH we understand that each of us keeps secret from others a large portion of who we are, much of the time we try to act as though we have nothing to hide. Of course, no one is expected to go out in public fully exposing his or her true self. That unadorned self is reserved for the private occasions of intimate meetings with trusted family members, personal friends, and selected lovers.

The mask worn by the social self is an attempt to live up to the community standards, to be the sort of person our family and friends expect us to be. Although these disguises may help us get through some of life's social situations more smoothly, like any impersonation they require our continued attention. The more often we wear a mask, and the less the mask is like our real self, the more vigilance is required, and the more of our valuable creative energy is used up to maintain the illusion that we are who we appear to be.

If we take off masks we have worn too long, some parts of our faces may come off with them.

A LIFE without purpose is an empty life. But to awake each morning with the first conscious thought, "Today is Monday," is to face the list of accomplishments an overachiever must undertake. Understanding that these obsessional thoughts are not rational will not make them go away.

Looking forward to a day off is no better. Instead we must face each day as it comes, do what we need to do, and take time out when we need to relax.

Curiously, the horrors of being reduced to some kind of infantile dependency may seem appealing. And although our nondisabling, garden-variety neurosis is moderately distressing, we don't have to go crazy before we are allowed to rest. That's no way to take a vacation.

The purpose of our existence is not to make a living but to make a life.

WHEN PEOPLE are excessively hopeful about future events, they consciously deny their own power in the present, even though control is a very important part of their unconscious intent. Wearing blinders, they deny their underlying fears and refuse to take on responsibility for their own happiness.

Hopeful, no matter what, these people glorify their powerlessness as if it were a virtue. They act as if God will watch over the weak and naive. Seeming to look to future rewards, excessively hopeful characters remain secretly preoccupied with the past, pretending that childhood is never outgrown and that they will always be watched over.

These folks range widely from pseudocompliant adults, always trying hard to be good children, to shamelessly reckless, righteous reformers bent on ultimate victory over the oppressive parents of the world. In the long run it doesn't much matter. The price for the protection these defenses offer is the limitation of personal and spiritual growth.

If we expect good fortune to take care of things, we are unlikely to take good care of ourselves.

EVEN THOUGH we may be aware of the risks of facing our hidden selves, simply knowing the dangers that lurk in the shadows has not been enough to enable us to peer into the darkness. Even during those times when we feel strong and safe enough to pursue finding out more about ourselves, we become confused and isolated. So, often we avoid risk by clinging to the limited, unexamined consciousness that accompanies our everyday experiences.

Sometimes our loneliness feels more bearable because of the support and instruction we receive from reading other people's tales of encountering what they see as negative in their hidden selves. Together we may yet learn to open our eyes more willingly to the expanded personal consciousness that makes accepting ourselves a real possibility.

Everyone has dreams of triumph and fantasies of humiliation.

October 17

WHEN WE deny that we really want to do what we think we shouldn't do, it can be difficult to maintain our idealized self-images. Sometimes we have to set aside the urges we feel as too earthy to be openly expressed, too savage to be even privately fantasized.

A good deal of psychic energy is consumed to hide or contain the parts of ourselves that we have been taught to disapprove of and so to disavow. The more rigidly divided we are, the more compulsive the vigilance required to ward off the threat of losing control. Yet, when we do slip from time to time, as we all must do, we feel publicly disgraced. Trying to discount or minimize the exposure, we only make ourselves look worse in the eyes of those we imagine are watching our every move.

When we realize how little what we do matters to other people, we feel more free to reveal our inner selves.

WHEN WE'VE buried our natural impulses and put a hold on our spontaneous feelings, we are not likely to have much fun. Nor are we likely to *be* much fun. Our humorless, effortful self-conscious manner leaves little space for lightness or spontaneity. Dignified and deliberate, we avoid or ignore our own simplest wishes for pleasure as temptations we don't deserve. We try to behave as we've been taught we should. We dare not do as we please. We might lose control, or even go crazy. Then everything could fall apart.

Paradoxically, the more we use our energy to maintain the illusion of being in control, the less in charge of our lives we actually are. With whatever energy remains, we try to match our attempts at keeping external order with an illusion of inner certainty. If only we carefully considered every alternative, says our imagination, then we could be sure that everything would turn out perfectly.

Unlived lives are not worth examining.

IN FRANZ Kafka's "Metamorphosis," the main character Gregor is transformed into a gigantic insect. This grotesque change surrealistically dramatizes just how foreign Gregor finds his own inner being. Gregor's alienation from the core of his personality is the result of living in a family in which no one knows who he is. They give the appearance of a concerned family and they maintain this illusion so successfully that no one recognizes that no one cares.

To protect himself against being overwhelmed by loneliness, Gregor goes along with the others, ignoring his longing to be personally valued for himself alone. He sacrifices having a personal self of his own and settles for becoming what others expect him to be.

Having lived most of his life as an impersonal false self, he fears that the emergence of the real one can only lead to total annihilation. Living an unbearably empty life, eventually he is reduced to feeling nothing more than a wish to die.

A self obsessively divided between illusion and reality is always a maintenance problem.

BEING CAUGHT unprepared makes us all vulnerable to being embarrassed. When the unexpected occurs, we're caught unaware, and if some particularly sensitive, intimate, or vulnerable aspect of ourselves is exposed, the pain is intense. The discrepancy between the completely coping person we assume we are and whom we hope others assume we are is now exposed as a blundering, vulnerable incompetent.

For that moment, all bets are off. Trust of self and others is in jeopardy. All values are once again in question. We begin to think: "Am I an adequate human being or a fool? What can I expect of myself? Do I really know what I am doing?"

We also feel compelled to question trust in the others who have witnessed our major-league blunder. Trust is the focus, especially when the embarrassment arises in the context of the rejected gift, the joke, or the phrase that does not come off: "Are these witnesses truly my friends? How do they really feel about me? If they once thought me capable, have they now lost faith in my abilities? I am left feeling helpless."

There is no way to be able to handle everything, no way to get it all just right all the time.

October 21

IT'S EASY to blame our parents for the real or imagined, intentional or unintentional ways they hurt us when we were too young to question the validity of the messages they gave us about our own self-worth. Once we become adults, they are no longer responsible for our personal journeys through life. Now the enemy is within.

We are the ones who shame ourselves now. We are the ones with overblown egos, arrogantly insisting that the same flaws we find acceptable in other people are unacceptable in ourselves.

If we stay stuck living the tediously painful life of the perfectionistic striver, we examine every move we make in the light of, "Was it good enough?" This is far too high a price to pay for maintaining the illusion that we might be able to rise above human frailty. As we try to make our way, we are certain to mess up again and again. We must make our inevitable mistakes, face our foolishness, forgive ourselves as best as we can, and go on.

Perfection is one goal that guarantees failure.

HOW ARE we to know what is real and freely chosen, what is here and now? For some people, checking on what others think helps. But even if everyone else believes we should act in a particular way, does conscience by committee result in right living?

Sorting out when we have options and when we do not is often difficult. Without any possibility of being certain of our assessments, we must learn to do the best we can and to find it sufficient. And when we have done all that we can, we must learn to give up and to forgive ourselves for not having been able to do more.

The option of lonely independence versus self-sacrificing conformity is only one of the polarities that we must each face completely on our own with only the higher power within each of us as a guide.

Making decisions on our own is better than allowing others to choose for us.

October 23

WHEN SOMEONE you care about hurts your feelings, it's difficult to drop your guard. The one who has struck the first blow might not have intended to be hurtful or may simply have underestimated how painful the experience might feel to the recipient.

When you feel hurt by a person whom you count on to treat you well, it's easy to imagine that the injury was inflicted deliberately and to be tempted to either fight back or withdraw.

An alternative that we often avoid is an open show of vulnerability. It takes trust and courage to risk simply saying, "When you talk to me that way, I feel hurt," especially if you say it without whining or being irritable. If we can begin by simply trying to be open and vulnerable, many hurtful experiences can avoid being repeated.

Revealing your vulnerability can have a powerful impact on others.

"EVERYONE GOT invited but me," the child sobbed in her mother's lap. The adult version of feeling betrayal occurs when someone says, "Oh, I'm so sorry! I never would have mentioned the party if I'd known you weren't invited—but I thought you two were good friends?"

Who can you depend on? Who can you trust? Whether the people in question are friends, lovers, or family, to risk becoming intimate and vulnerable with another human being is to risk disappointment, rejection, and abandonment. These are big risks, but with varying degrees of possibility and pain.

With friends and potential lovers, you may be well advised to take little steps into the shallow end of the pool, testing the waters, before you plunge into the deep end and reveal your most sacred secrets. But eventually, after time and good sense have prevailed, you have to risk intimacy. You must be willing to try and to risk feeling the pain, because the empty alternative hurts much worse.

Without trust, we can't accept the intimacy of gently holding another's trembling heart in our hands, or placing ours in theirs.

THERE'S ONE sure way to live in the present and that is to have no past or future. In the language of the Hopi Indians, for instance, life in the eternal present is reflected by an absence of past, present, and future tenses. Words for seasons, whether winter or summer, are not nouns that indicate separate sections of time. They are descriptive words, reflecting the condition of the continuous but also changing nature of the present time.

Life transitions for the Hopi are also unmarked by the strict time divisions of our chronological categories. In our culture, one minute we are single and free of family responsibility, but the moment after our wedding we are committed for life to one person and the children we'll bear. In the Hopi culture, marriage includes more than two dozen events spaced out over an entire year.

The value of understanding the Hopi way is, in part, so those of us who tend to ignore what is going on right now can get our attention off the horizon and on to watching where we are.

Whatever we are undertaking at the moment is the most important thing we can do.

NO ONE is ever totally safe from harm. No matter how cautiously we live our lives, occasionally we will get physically or emotionally hurt. Knowing and anticipating this, we may suffer anxiety, continually worrying about what terror will strike next. Hoping to avoid calamity, we cling to familiar patterns that seem secure. Even so, we remain afraid.

Instead of living constantly afraid, we can find some comfort in the act of turning toward our fear. Courage is not the absence of fear but the ability to face its presence. Running scared is much like trying to cross an unfamiliar room in the dark. When we turn the light on first, we learn what the obstacles are.

Independence isn't living without support from others; it is developing the capacity to adequately care for ourselves instead of childishly clinging to others for protection. With some courage and independence we can indulge in curiosity and improvise a colorful, adventuresome lifestyle, all without putting ourselves needlessly and recklessly at risk.

Facing our fears saves us from suffering needless anxieties.

FEELING LIKE "a nothing" hurts. You go through feelings of being a nothing, a person without purpose or direction, especially when you've suffered a big loss or when there's a major transition in your life.

For example if you lose your job, you feel devalued. One minute you were a person with a position, gainfully employed, successful, probably supporting others, and the next minute, all these labels are stripped from you. If you're a mother and your last child has left home, you may have the sense of losing not only your job but also your identity.

During these difficult transition times, you have to begin again to define clearly who you really are. Some transitions are very painful, especially if the change involves loss of a loved one through death or divorce. There is work to do and grieving to endure. Then it's back to square one and you must make a new beginning.

Even though some losses are irreplaceable, we must find ways to move on.

IRONICALLY, MANY important things in our lives are most clearly defined by what they aren't, rather than by what they are; or they are best appreciated when we don't have them anymore. Health is a good example. Usually you don't wake up thinking, "I'm so glad I feel well today." But on those days you wake up feeling ill, you know that the best times were and will be when you're feeling well again.

Minor contrasts and major catastrophes happen as a part of life, but out of the changes can come value. Without change, without disruption, some good and some bad, everything would be the same. We won't know peace and happiness if we can only experience one way of being.

Unless we recognize that ups and downs are going to happen, we may easily spend our entire lives as passive reactors, instead of actively going forward in our uniquely chosen directions. Unless we realize that we can't wait to live until everything is in order, we'll end up asking ourselves as Rabbi Kushner did, "Was there something I was supposed to do with my life?"

We have to play the hand we've been dealt.

October 29

WE MAKE a mistake when we believe that we must continually give up our own wants and needs in order to love others. There are times of sacrifice to be sure, but loving others does not imply a life of selfless service.

When one spiritual teacher found that a guest at his table had not begun to eat with the others, he asked the man why. The guest humbly replied that he had no spoon. "Look," said the teacher, "you must know enough to ask for a spoon, and a plate, too, if need be!"

If we try to live a life of self-sacrifice and personal denial, most of us will soon demand attention for being martyrs or blame others for making us victims. And, as Drs. Jordan and Margaret Paul explain in *Do I Have to Give Up Me to Be Loved by You?*, if our loving behavior compromises our own personal growth, most likely our intent is not to give love but to get love for ourselves.

We treat our loved ones well by taking good care of ourselves.

OUR RELUCTANCE to accept being on our own is understandable. Learning that we have to take care of ourselves is one of the more painful losses of innocence. But, as adults, we can still count on others to look after us some of the time. Someone else may attend to our needs as an act of love or kindness, or simply because their services are for hire. But our well-being is rarely (if ever) as fundamentally important to anyone else as their own.

Too much care is not a help to anyone. Unfortunately, many personal and professional caretakers are unconsciously focused on filling their own unmet needs for care. As a result, the real needs of those in their care—children, spouses, patients—are disregarded.

The best nurturing support and healthy helping is reliable, but not chronic. When the caretaker allows some options for self-reliance, the cared for end up better able to take care of themselves.

Trying to fix your broken places by repairing someone else can cause both of you a lot of harm.

MANY WAYS that people take care of one another are useful and trustworthy. Caretaking can start out as reliable, competent, and unselfish. But anyone who assumes a position of being responsible for another is subject to the corrupting temptations that come with that power.

It is difficult to take responsibility for other people's well-being without beginning to believe that we know what is best for them. The very need for care seems to discredit their competence or even a right to live their own lives.

When caretaking also implies a position of power or control over another person, the ones in charge would be well advised to question their motives. And, those who continue to be submissive would do well to wonder why they want to let someone else direct their lives.

Neither a jailer nor a prisoner be.

IN THE old Hasidic "Story of the Cape," a woman went to a rabbi, saying tearfully she'd been married many years, but still hadn't borne a baby. "What are you willing to do about it?" he asked her. She didn't know what to say.

"My mother," the rabbi said, "was aging and still had no child. Hearing that a holy man had stopped nearby, she hurried to his inn and begged him to pray she might bear a son."

"What are you willing to do about it?" he asked. She was very poor but she had one fine thing, a cape. She went home, fetched her good cape to offer him, but the holy teacher had already left. So, she set out after him, walking from town to town until she found him. He took the cape, hung it on the wall, and said, "It is well." My mother walked all the way back home. A year later, I was born.

"I, too, will bring you a cape," cried the woman, "so I may have a son."

"That won't work," said the rabbi. "You heard my mother's tale. She had to create her own story."

At each crossroad, we must take a path of our own choosing.

November 2

WE CAN'T spend our lives reasonably safe from harm hiding under the covers because we're afraid of the dark. How can we learn to distinguish when it's appropriate to be afraid and when we are safe to remain at ease?

For one thing, we must make certain that when we avoid risk, we do so out of our own fear of what might harm us, rather than out of anxiety that we'll be making someone else uneasy. Then we must take the responsibility for deciding whether the rewards of taking—or avoiding—a particular action are worth the risk.

Unless we learn to recognize risk in personal terms and are willing to decide for ourselves and act on our own, we sacrifice the option of doing as we please. Otherwise we have to settle for walking the narrow path between others' approval and the deceptive deadliness of their disapproval.

If you don't play, you won't lose, but you can't win.

BUMPER STICKERS are an interesting phenomenon. They've become a way for drivers to broadcast their own brief message to the world. Although stickers are probably bought with a sense of humor, still they allow the drivers to display an image of themselves for all to see. A few samples are:

> *"Life's a bitch, then you die."*
> *"I brake for hallucinations."*
> *"The one who dies with the most toys wins."*
> *"Are we having fun yet?"*
> *"I refuse to grow up."*

Psychiatrist Dr. Joseph Pursch, well known for his work in the treatment of addiction, reports seeing one sticker that made a public confession: "My other car went up my nose."

A few stickers give advice we can all use in our own ways. "Take it easy" is one. "Turn it over" is another.

When you identify yourself, be sure you use your right name.

November 4

"THE ONLY trouble with my life is that none of it makes any sense. I've always felt more dead than alive." If this is your complaint, then typically your unexpressed fear would be, "What if this means I'm really crazy?" or "What if in trying to find a self of my own, I discover that, like an onion, once all my outer layers are peeled away, there is nothing left?"

Self-examination may feel like peering into a black hole in deep space. Fortunately, in seeking the center of your self, you will find no dreaded bottomless pit of emptiness and the monsters you fear will be only passing sights.

If you come to accept this and still refuse to turn and look within, could it be you fear that what you'll learn is that you are no different than anyone else? If you accept your ordinariness, you will also have to give up your harbored notion of being special. But, in place of superiority is your genuine, precious uniqueness, which like love, cannot be earned, won, or lost. It is your personal treasure and the foundation on which to build the home that is your character.

Making an inner journey is risky business—it can transform your life.

SOME PEOPLE would settle for little more in life than an explanation for their unhappiness. It would all seem bearable, perhaps even worthwhile, if only somehow they could make sense of their suffering. They try to make up reasons to account for their unhappiness.

Surely their childhood had a lot to do with the mess they're in, but even that doesn't provide a satisfactory explanation. There must be someone wiser than they are who knows the answers. If only they could attach themselves to someone who knew the true meaning of life, a magic helper who could be depended on to look after them, then their worries would finally end.

Some part of us longs for assurance that we don't have to worry because there will be someone to look after us. This longing to be rescued from our struggles is a temptation against which we must continue to struggle every day for the rest of our lives.

Sometimes we need to stop crying for help and get on with getting ourselves unstuck.

November 6

IN HIS topsy-turvy tale, *Alice's Adventures in Wonderland*, Lewis Carroll explores the underside of life in the chaos of Wonderland, where "everything's got a moral if only you can find it." Adults almost inevitably find that Wonderland is like life. The comically absurd situations give us a chance to laugh, which we must all do at times or die of despair.

When Alice follows the White Rabbit down the rabbit hole, she is plunged into a place where nothing, including language, works in a familiar way. Even the traditional dimensions of orderly time and space are nowhere to be found. Desperately reciting memorized lessons, she tries to make sense of the present chaos in terms of the stable past. When Alice can no longer count on her beliefs to make sense, she first loses her security and then her identity, asking throughout her adventures, "But then . . . who am I?"

Like Alice, as we face our own disorganized world, we're tempted to escape back into the reassuring innocence of childhood. Choosing to act unhampered by conventional wisdom gives us greater freedom. Still, that freedom is hard to hold onto. We have to trust ourselves even when everyone else seems to agree that we don't know what we're doing.

There are times when your freedom depends on believing in yourself, no matter what anyone else thinks.

FROM TIME to time, all of us get tired of taking care of ourselves. When we're stressed or unhappy, we especially need a chance to be taken care of as if we were a child.

At the end of a long, difficult day, how good it is to return home to someone who cares about how we feel! Like a child, we can come to them for parenting, and like a mother or father, they can take us in. It's the sort of momentary comfort that may get both partners through life.

Rather than actually trying to fix the other's feelings, the one fulfilling the role of parent needs to be available to listen to feelings and communicate, "I'm here and I care. I'm sorry you're having such a tough time. I'm willing to hurt because you hurt, and to be respectfully careful not to tell you how you should feel or what you should do."

If this can happen without the two forgetting they are adults, then tonight's pretend parent can be tomorrow night's pretend child.

Comforting each other is not just child's play.

November 8

THE DESERT Fathers, those early Christian spiritual pilgrims, retreated to caves to be alone with their thoughts, but irony pervaded their tradition of solitude. The monks sought the solitude of the desert as a way of seeking to confront God, one to One. Yet, through this experience, they became aware that "the giant agony of the world" couldn't be ignored. Anthony, one of the first of these hermits, said, "With our neighbor is life and death."

A life of solitude in a cell was not for those who weren't ready. Another abbot, Abba Lucius, said that men must amend their lives among other people before they can be ready to dwell alone.

The seeking of salvation is more a state of mind and spirit than physical setting. And so it was also said, "It is better to have many about you and to live the solitary life in your will, than to be alone and have your mind's desire be with the crowd."

Take your stand by being where you are.

IN CHOOSING to display to others only what fits the public image we hope for, we have to watch what we do and what we say. Posing in this way robs us of spontaneity and deprives us of new experiences. Ironically, when we conceal our vulnerability and avoid the risk of lowered self-esteem, we may miss out on opportunities to increase our feelings of self-worth. Misguided efforts at protecting our image can diminish how much more we might value who we are.

There are times when we may have no other option than to divide parts of our selves and hide them away, but even then the constraints required are scarcely worth the safety gained. Once revealed, our darker sides can be transformed by exposure to the light.

We all juggle too many selves. Life sometimes seems a poorly constructed masquerade that exposes what we hoped to hide. We have to learn to live with some of the contradictions between our revealed and our concealed selves. Otherwise, the discrepancy and the inconsistency make us feel like frauds, acting our way through unreal experiences in meaningless lives.

It's hard to enjoy life when you're watching it from over your own shoulder.

RELATIONSHIPS WITH others always challenge us to work through conflict. At those times, it's hard to remain sensible and unselfish. If we acknowledge and accept all the awful, hidden parts of ourselves, it seems that we would create even more difficulties with other people. Actually, the opposite is true.

Identifying our unthinkable aspects need not involve indulging them. Once we recognize these peculiarities, we are better able to prevent them from negatively affecting our relationships. The more we accept our awful aspects, the less we project them on others. When we stop using other people as containers for the unacceptable parts of our self, we give up denying how disappointing, inconsistent, imperfect, and inadequate our own personality has seemed to us.

If, instead, we expand our idealized self-images to include all we might wish we weren't, then we can treat other people with the respect due their wholly separate souls.

When we make ourselves feel better by diminishing other people we leave little room for mutually respectful relationships.

SHIVA, THE Hindu god of contradictions, not only carries fiery arrows and a bow but healing remedies as well. A fierce intermediary of the inevitable disruptions in life, he teaches us how to heal the very wounds he inflicts.

Like other male Hindu gods, Shiva has a feminine aspect that takes many forms. As Kali, she acts as the indifferently devouring mother of sorrows who exhausts and ages us all. Utterly indiscriminating as the feminine form of Time, she challenges our arrogant egos and gradually wears us down with the impersonal necessities of everyday living.

Like life itself, whether fierce or friendly, Kali is entirely unpredictable. It is as impossible to prepare for her coming as it is to control her once she arrives. One minute we are prosperous and peaceful; the next we are sick or battered by unexpected disappointment. She makes us aware that we can't manage life's onslaughts. Neither reason nor right and wrong can rein in her ravages. Kali reminds us that no one can escape the untamed, uncaring, uncompromising force of Time.

Accept your losses or you'll get no gains.

November 12

THERE IS no ultimate way to distinguish what is real from what we have imagined. We may find others who agree with us, but when a particular person sees it one way and others disagree, what are we to do? Either we must turn to some imperfect, appointed authority, or we must decide for ourselves what is real and what is not.

Usually we are confident that we can judge with certainty whether an experience "actually happened" or we were "only dreaming." However, if we can't tell for sure, then not knowing the boundary between what is real and unreal is confusing and can be terrifying. It is understandable that we insist on continually renewing our all-or-nothing distinctions between true and false, good and bad, crazy and sane, and between dreaming and waking.

It is our responsibility to recognize what reality is for us.

IF SOMEONE asks you to "Please pass the salt," there is very little room for misunderstanding. However, if you're asked, "What do you think you really mean by what you just seemed to say?" all at once, it is no longer a simple matter of this or that, yes or no.

Our subjective interpretations are particularly affected by intense emotions. Even subtle hopes and fears influence how we see things and the ways we interpret facts to fit attitudes.

In circumstances that are highly emotional and/or subjective, we usually still assume that there is only one true reality. However, if this delusion of a true reality remains unexamined, we come to believe that surely our own personal experience is right. If others disagree, they must be fools or liars. Given the way our minds naturally work, it's a wonder we're able to agree with each other at all.

All we know is what we imagine to be true.

November 14

NO MATTER how well defined or strongly supported, our civilized veneer remains thin and tentative. Hidden within each of us is an animal driven by uncivilized impulses that activate instinctual patterns of mating, fighting, playing, and seeking power.

Usually we'd much rather view our interactions as expressions of higher sentiments and noble principles, but at times our behavior is a display of territorial imperatives and other unwitting biological patterns, and aggressive animal instincts. Often we act like the animals we are. In many instances, our only significantly "higher" human expressions consist of the ways we hide or explain away our base urges.

Like the tentative encounters of animals in a forest, our meetings with other people are highly sensitized interactions that are often uneasy. The mere entering and leaving of each other's space always involves some instinctive territorial response of invading or being invaded, of abandoning or being abandoned. Many of our ritual conversations express good will to ease these tensions.

The beast within us can be held in check, but we can never tame it completely.

IF WE were to awake and immediately think, "It's the weekend," we'd know that our work is finished for the week and that we could rest. But if we were really, truly relaxed it would mean waking up without immediately having to decide what day it was, and understanding that it was up to us to choose to work or play as we pleased. The point is not whether or not the thought is realistic in terms of choices we have to make but how our subconsciousness is organized around the thoughts of what we have to do.

Some of us worry about working hard enough because our need to achieve is all that justifies allowing ourselves to take a vacation. That alone is difficult to bear. But another subset of us compulsive achievers works hard enough to prove that we are worthwhile human beings. The downside to this driven path is that our imagination tells us that we would have to go crazy, have a nervous breakdown, or get seriously ill in order to have any rest. This is burden enough to tire us so that we should go back to sleep.

If you need proof that you are entitled to rest, you may never feel okay about taking it easy.

BEFORE WE are free to enjoy what we can of life, we must face the seemingly unbearable frustration of trying to make life work the way we imagine it should. Often happiness depends on giving up our idealized vision of a logical world with predictable results. Usually we take our illusions too seriously by imagining that they are the true reality.

These paradoxes cannot be resolved. Much of life is predictably unpredictable, intrinsically incoherent, and finally full of surprises. Ambiguity is unending. We must willingly imagine simultaneously both our hopes and our fears, the ideal and the practical, the absolute and the relative, other people's way of looking at things and our own.

One way is often as good as another. Perhaps most crucial is that we each be allowed to imagine things our way and that we allow others to live their own way. What works for one of us doesn't necessarily work for the other.

"I will save you from drowning," said the bird, as it lifted the fish up out of the water to place it safely in a tree.

IN AN old tale, "The Bull and the Maze," a certain people believed that eating the flesh of a bull would make men powerful and fearless. Since the animal was considered sacred and its killing forbidden, they would trick a bull into killing himself.

Complicated wooden mazes were built with solid concrete walls behind them, low enough for the bull to see the pastures on the other side, but high enough to prevent him from jumping over. Trapped in the maze, a bull would eventually batter at the back wall until he killed himself. He would hate the wall for being there. He would hate it for not succumbing to his strength and fearlessness. His anger at this wall would reinforce itself and his efforts to knock it down would take on a personal vengeance, compelling him to continue to batter and at the same time continue to beat his brains out. Unfortunately, the bull never understood that the wall couldn't hurt him unless he ran into it.

Who has ever given us as much trouble as we have given ourselves?

November 18

WHEN WE want to do something we know is dangerous, we're more likely to rationalize it with a statement like "I know nothing bad will happen today," than to say, "I know that driving too fast is risky, but I want so much to see how fast my new car can go that I'll accept the risk." Ironically, when we insist we'll be safe in this way, our magical thinking actually increases our probability of being harmed.

We are also willing to accept greater risks in areas where we imagine we are in command than others that seem out of our control. For example, we might be willing to be less cautious driving a car than flying a plane.

From time to time, we all experience terror in the absence of actual threat. In such situations, we need to keep in mind that no matter how irrational we may know the fear to be, we need to treat our feelings with respect. We may wake in the night in a cold sweat, terrified that we are about to die. Even though we know that the danger is only in our imagination, facing the fear may allow us to ask someone we love to hold and comfort us until the terror passes.

Even when you know there is no real danger, you mustn't ignore feeling afraid.

A TEENAGER will take on risks to make an experience more exciting and real, while worldly wise and weary adults avoid risk, letting caution restrict their lives. Forgetting their own youthful ways, the grown-ups rationalize, "This is the way we've always done things."

Young innocents live in a timeless state, only interested in *now*. Knowing all and needing nothing, they are as self-absorbed as their elders. The older ones are sure of already knowing the answers that youth search for, while the young people are as dogmatic as the authority they rebel against.

Youth and age are simultaneously very similar and very different. Both are misled by their emotions: Youth is moody; age is melancholy. Both believe they are absolutely right and both resist change, yet the younger ones cut corners without compunction, while the older generation compulsively insists on doing things the right way. While they remain at odds, neither can recognize that the old were once young and that the young will someday be old.

 A wise elder with many children once said, "Now that I know the answers, no one asks me the questions."

November 20

CULTS ARE attractive to many, especially young people, because a cult offers freedom from uncertainty. As one young man put it, "I love it. No more decisions to make." Depending on the kind of cult and the setup of communal living, you may not even have to decide what to do with your time. Furthermore, now that you belong, you can depend on the group to take care of your needs. No more struggles, no worries, just peace. Join the club and you're guaranteed a ticket to heaven, so the promise goes.

Utopia on earth and heaven thereafter sounds too good to be true. To paraphrase Jung, when you live as a "herd-being," in this case, a cult member, you have no "things of the spirit" of your own. No individual mind, no personal life. Wounded and needy people, afraid, vulnerable, alone, and often young are the ones who have bought into the concept, but probably without realizing, they have traded life on earth for death in life.

Sometimes the cure can be worse than the disease.

AT TIMES when we feel desperate and helpless, some of us are tempted to stubbornly insist on having things our own way. By then, we don't care anymore whether or not what we want at that moment suits our overall goals. Demonically, our will acts as if it had a life of its own, separate from the purpose we pursue or from our larger picture of the greater good.

All we know is that we won't give in, no matter what! Spitefully, we may simply settle for our opponent not getting his or her way, apart from any gain or loss that may result for us.

Total commitment to fighting for what we want can accomplish worthwhile ends but only if it serves as an act of devotion. When we act out of desperation, we risk becoming fanatics. As George Santayana wrote, "Fanaticism consists in redoubling your effort when you have forgotten your aim."

Getting our own way may not always be the best thing for us.

November 22

A HOLY man once had an apprentice who worked very hard for him. As a matter of fact, the master only kept him because of his great effort, since otherwise he thought the apprentice was rather stupid.

One day, a rumor spread that the apprentice had walked on water, crossing a river as easily as if he were crossing a street. The master questioned him, "Is this true? Can you really cross the river by walking on the water?"

"Ah, yes," the apprentice replied, "thanks to you. Every step of the way I repeat your saintly name and that is what holds me up."

The holy man thought to himself, "If it is in my name that this miracle occurs, I must possess power I did not suspect. But, after all, I have never tried it."

So, the master hurried to the river, stepped off the bank onto the water, chanting with complete faith, "Me, me, me." And he sank.

A touch of humility helps us find our way.

WE ARE all tempted to escape life's woes. Some of us watch television, go bowling, do crossword puzzles, or play arcade games. Idealistic elders in the community tell us that we are being frivolous and wasting time that could be put to better use. They tell us that we are escapists who are unwilling to face reality.

Certainly, there are those who seek to avoid life's difficulties and pain by sedating their pain with alcohol and drugs, or who turn off their minds when they turn on television. A life spent entirely in escapism is a life unlived. But there are times when we need to lighten up and give ourselves a break.

As Peter Cook put it, "I go to the theater to be entertained. . . . I don't want to see plays about rape, sodomy and drug addiction. . . . I can get all that at home."

Escape *is not a dirty word. You can't face life head on all the time.*

November 24

WHEN WE try too hard to hold on to something we value, we are very likely to lose it. Possessive jealousy destroys love, fear of aging distracts us from enjoying youth, and worrying about how some experience will end keeps us from enjoying how it is going at the moment.

The Buddha taught that all suffering is the result of attachment. We only get to keep what we are willing to let go. When we concentrate on trying to hold on to pleasure, we keep ourselves from experiencing all that the moment has to offer, just as fussing about pain gets in the way of experiencing relief.

Enjoyment of what we have is lost by longing for what we haven't got. As Aldous Huxley tells us, "Only the ephemeral is of lasting value."

Let it go, or lose it.

WHEN SOMEONE tells us that we've hurt their feelings, it can be difficult to tell if we've actually done them emotional damage. When what we've said is a betrayal of our personal commitment to treating them well, we are responsible for having hurt them. But, if it is simply our choice of words that offends some social standard they believe everyone should live up to, then it is *their reaction* to what we've said that is causing them pain.

Social standards for behavior have their own importance, but we should not confuse manners with morals. When we teach our children formal table manners, it allows them both the tool of following the rules when they want to comply for political purposes and the weapon of breaking the rules when they want to rebel.

To be effective in the world, we need to learn not to hurt others' feelings by accident.

November 26

WAKING UP depressed feels awful, so we may try to distract ourselves by escaping into superficial entertainments or immersing ourselves in busywork. Although we may feel relieved temporarily, the depression soon returns. Often our morning moodiness is the residual of a bad dream we're trying to forget, an inner voice inviting our attention to a worry we're attempting to ignore. When we willingly accept our depression as an indication that we're not facing something unpleasant, the underlying problem can become painfully clear.

Bad as it feels, depression is a gift. It causes us to take time out of our routine and begin the task of attending to the problem we've been trying to avoid.

To do this soulwork, you must begin by understanding that you are not your depression—that you are not a problem; you simply have a problem to solve. Also, you must be willing to stay depressed for a while without either pulling away from the feeling or passively suffering while waiting for the mood to pass. If you don't want to live a life haunted by hidden depression, you must accept the opportunity for reflection that your moodiness provides. To recover and to grow, you must take the path that leads down and in.

Make the most of depression. It's not simple, though, and it's not easy, but it helps us realize we need to make changes.

HARD AND fast rules give us the false self-assurance that with these pearls of wisdom we will know what is right in every situation. We pay an exorbitant price for this costume-jewelry confidence that fools us into believing that we can count on these seemingly unflawed gems as a solution for every problem.

Of course, life is too fluid and impermanent for rigid ideas of morality. This ambiguity and variation is more apparent when we are dealing with other people. As pediatrician Benjamin Spock reminds us, "How to fold a diaper depends on the size of the baby and the diaper."

Also, no matter how conscientious we are, none of us is entirely free of wrongdoing. Who among us can claim to be without temptation? And, given few if any absolute moral laws, how are we to know right from wrong? Hemingway suggests that, "What is moral is what you feel good after and what is immoral is what you feel bad after."

To discover ways for right living, we must look to the context for clues.

November 28

WHEN WE meet people for the first time, we often begin to try to get to know them by asking what they do for a living. Even if no one has asked us, we may try to identify ourselves by naming our occupation.

Knowing the work we do sometimes serves to stake out common interests. More often it simply allows us to categorize each other in ways that are familiar, but impersonal and often inaccurate.

It may be awkward, but it's often rewarding to ask, "Who are you when you're not an engineer (or a shop-keeper, or a salesperson)?" Common interests are a sound basis for hobby clubs and activity groups, but in personal relationships, the bedrock is our reciprocal interest in getting to know each other.

We are all more than the labels assigned to us.

PEOPLE'S BELIEF in God ranges from militant atheism to devout faith. Variations of belief in what God has in mind may be even more varied than in whether or not He or She exists.

The crucial issue is that the human psyche needs some sort of relationship with a higher power, whether within or without, benign or malignant, merciful or just, or simply Someone whose existence they find important to deny. As Luis Buñuel said, "I am an atheist, still, thank God."

Whether or not we have faith does not determine
God's existence.

IN SOME families, two members will form an alliance and gossip about a third. This mock intimacy effectively excludes the other family member. The allied "good guys" seldom realize that it will soon be their turn to be the scapegoats.

When someone in your family offers you the temptation to pair off in this sort of exclusive, mutual admiration pact, think twice before accepting the invitation. Instead, you can simply say, "I'm sorry you're troubled about that relationship, but that's none of my business. Why don't you talk to him (or her) about what's bothering you?"

Alliances formed by two people to exclude a third amount to heartbreaking affairs of make-believe love.

In *Brave New World,* first published in 1932, visionary Aldous Huxley described a Utopian society where babies were all genetically engineered so their intellects suited their level of work and all were conditioned to be happy with their lot. The appalling dangers of family life had been revealed by their god, Our Ford, back when the "world was full of fathers . . . full of mothers . . . full of madness and suicide." Only a few savages from that time remained and they had been exiled to distant reservations.

When one Savage met some Utopian citizens, he was taught about their perfect society and its complete comfort, lack of violence, and happiness as the Sovereign Good. In the end the Savage reacted strongly against the Utopia: "But I don't want comfort. . . . I want real danger. I want freedom, I want goodness, I want sin."

"In fact," was the response, "you're claiming the right to be unhappy."

"Not to mention the right to grow old and ugly and impotent . . . the right to live in constant apprehension of what may happen tomorrow," he answered.

Protection from life's worst pains costs us the freedom to experience its greatest pleasures.

December 2

WHEN WE'VE had a serious illness or injury and a brush with death, we become intensely aware of the people we love and have a renewed sense of what is and isn't important in our lives. Although we're certain that we'll continually remain aware of our new perspective, after time the impact fades. Little by little, we begin again to take our lives and our loved ones for granted. Dr. Oliver Sacks, psychiatrist and author of *The Man Who Mistook His Wife for a Hat*, cautions us to "beware of the arrogance of health."

How can we keep the learning without going again to life's edge for another lesson? Practice love is one answer. For Dr. Sacks that means continued work with difficult patients. The rest of us might gain insight from some well-worn slogans used in Alcoholics Anonymous:

"It's a pity we can't forget our troubles the same way we forget our blessings."
"To keep it, you have to give it away."
"Get it. Give it. Grow in it."

If we listen, life will teach us all we need to know.

WHEN A learned professor visited a Zen master, the professor began telling the master everything he knew about Zen philosophy. The professor continued to speak, while the master said nothing, but continued to pour tea into the professor's cup.

The professor talked on and on until he suddenly realized that the Zen master was still pouring tea, even though the cup had long since overflowed. "How can I add anything more to your great store of knowledge?" the master asked. "Like the tea cup, your mind is already full."

A poster portrays a beautiful forest with deep green foliage, tall trees, clear blue sky above, and down the center of the picture is a narrow but open path of warm-brown earth. A solitary runner with a studied but serene expression lopes along the path. The poster's caption: "There is no finish line."

Krishnamurti reflects: "Learning is not the accumulation of knowledge. Learning is movement from moment to moment."

The traveling and the sense of arrival are the same.

December 4

SOME PEOPLE are very attentive to other people's needs. They pride themselves on intuiting what is needed and providing it without having to be asked. More often than they imagine, they are experienced and intrusive and controlling.

The corollary of their "generosity" is that on the few occasions that they themselves feel needy they expect others to do the same for them. Often they are needlessly disappointed, as though the fact that a friend cannot read their mind means he (or she) doesn't really love them. Ironically, their attempt to avoid being a bother may make impossible demands on people who would be happy to help out if only they understood what was needed.

It's a lovely feeling when someone who cares about you understands and provides what you need without having to be asked, but sometimes you have to ask for what you want—sometimes more than once.

Loving me doesn't mean you have to be able to read my mind.

THE DEATH of a loved one is a painful aching in the chest, sobbed out in fragments. And just when you are sure that you've finished grieving once and for all, you turn an unexpected corner and run into another chunk of longing.

Facing our own death is very different from witnessing anyone else's. Without knowing when or how we'll die, we only know for sure that we will. The uncertainty is painful. Even more painful is thinking about giving up everyone and everything we love.

When it comes to dying, we are helplessly out of control. The only reasonable thing we can do is turn toward enjoying life as it has been given to us, by being as much ourselves as we are able, and by giving ourselves over to the pleasure of being with people we love and doing things that have meaning to us. We have to take what we can get and make of it what we can.

Like life, death makes fools of us all.

December 6

WHEN WE feel too scared to face fear on our own, we are tempted to seek the protection that comes from belonging to a social group. Immersing our individual identities in the collective image distracts us from our personal anxieties, but then we take on the fears of the group.

To our surprise, we discover that joining the crowd means it is now *us* against *them*, the outsiders. This is a high price to pay for safety in numbers. Those excluded by the group are deemed undesirable or dangerous. We may need to keep *them* in their place, whether they're radicals, the uneducated, the poor, or our own teenagers. We've become modern-day vigilantes who no longer form lynch mobs, but still we seek scapegoats. We can blame the victims and then *we* shall fear no evil because it was not our fault. It's our new way of feeling secure.

Sometimes, as individuals, we have good reason to feel afraid, but the risk of facing our fear alone must be weighed against sacrificing our scared selves to the terrifying reassurance of a group.

When we join a group only for security, the best we can hope for is trading one set of fears for another.

SOME PEOPLE dismiss compliments and discourage offers of help. Their protests clearly sound a false note, since it's obvious to others that their martyred stance is another way of attracting attention. Other people refuse credit more honestly, thinking that their exaggerated self-sufficiency is a way of diminishing demands on other people.

If you act this way, you ignore the possibility that the other people might enjoy expressing their admiration or giving you a hand. Rather than experiencing you as not wanting to be a bother, others may feel that their appreciation and reciprocation are being rejected.

All things considered, we don't need false modesty.

December 8

IN HINDU mythology, Vishnu descends to earth to defeat the demonic forces that disrupt the moral order and easy living. At times, the demons represent the dark, personally unloving aspects of our attitudes and actions toward each other that cause unnecessary human suffering. Mainly they simply stand for the random calamities that life imposes as indifferent necessities of misfortune marked "To whom it may concern."

As preserver of moral order, Vishnu comes to protect our physical and emotional well-being. Ready to offer himself in opposition to the demons, he is eternally on call to rescue those whose welfare he cherishes. His ever-changing incarnations are not expressions of his own needs but of his response to the neediness of those he loves.

When people we care about are in trouble, it may be time to put their needs ahead of our own.

THE EXPERIENCES of spiritual pilgrimages throughout history have much to offer us as we take our own steps on our personal journey. A person's efforts are both as real and as momentary as the lovely sand castles little children build too near the water's edge. In this marginal world of ever-changing, never-changing nature, we often lose sight of the original intent. How much wiser to let nature flow through us than to try to separate ourselves to stand against it. No one lives forever. No one can stand against the tide.

If we try to hold on to the past, then we will only fall more quickly and with less grace. We may get what we can from our own present efforts to struggle with what human happiness is all about, but only if we know that nothing lasts and if we accept our losses. We must give up what cannot last and what we cannot change if we are to have all we might of present meanings and today's joys.

We make everyday life holy when we are responsible for that bit of existence God has entrusted to our care.

December 10

WE OFTEN hear people say, "My parents (or friends, or partners) love me *in their own way.*" This insistence on believing that we are loved in the absence of experiencing the other as treating us lovingly is an empty illusion.

We want so badly to feel loved that we accept the good intentions of others as implications that they are attentive to what we need. Our stubborn insistence may feel reassuring, but it doesn't keep us warm at night.

If the only reason we know that someone loves us is because they say so, our relationship is in trouble. Affection is not a matter of policy statements.

Being loved is something we must experience in our hearts, not a matter to figure out in our heads.

SOME PEOPLE complain of helplessness, insisting that they don't take better care of themselves because they don't know how. Often, there are obvious contradictions in their claimed handicaps. For example, people who claim that they simply can't express themselves well in words may be far more articulate in describing their deficiencies than in speaking of their accomplishments.

Underlying these disparities is the fear that if they demonstrate just once how well they can manage on their own, the people they depend on will abandon them forever, leaving them to fend for themselves, no matter how difficult their circumstances.

Just because you can be self-sufficient some of the time does not mean that no one will help you when you aren't.

December 12

WE MUST learn to forgive ourselves for the occasional mistakes we make. This is particularly difficult when our error in judgment results in needlessly allowing someone else to take advantage of us. We can get caught in the push and pull of alternately blaming the perpetrator for being so cruel or blaming ourselves for having been so stupid.

In retrospect, we may realize that when we first met our oppressor, we sensed something in his or her attitude that we did not trust. For one reason or another, whether out of false hopes or unwarranted fear, we ignored our initial intuitive distrust. And now, we have paid by enduring mistreatment that we might have avoided.

Obsessing over a single misguided decision makes us more wary, but it also undermines our self-confidence. However, if we make the same sort of mistake by leaving ourselves open to repeated injury by the same uncaring partner, or by choosing to replace one unreliable partner with another, we might well examine our own poor track record more carefully.

Hurt me once, shame on you! Hurt me twice, shame on me!

IF ANYONE asks us why we love a particular person, we might be able to name some of the qualities, attitudes, and actions that we find especially endearing, but the sum of those traits does not add up to why we feel the love we do. There are people who have the same pleasing attributes whom we do not love, but only like or admire. Apart from those appealing traits, we may actually dislike some of them.

When we say we love someone, we mean that having them in our lives makes us happy. Telling our beloved "I love you" may simply be a way of expressing our joy. Nonetheless, saying it once and letting it go at that is a mistake. It's a feeling worth celebrating again and again.

If our love is deep, words cannot communicate the intensity of that tenderness as clearly as how lovingly we treat those we care about. As Buckminster Fuller said, "Love is a verb."

Don't settle for saying "I love you" without showing how much you care.

December 14

MANY COUPLES make what they think is a commitment to a monogamous relationship. Usually what they mean is, "I am committed to refrain from a romantic or sexual involvement with anyone else—so long as my partner keeps me happy, or unless I meet someone irresistible." The promise they make to themselves and/or to their mate often is meant to be sincere, but the conditional clauses undermine the validity of the contract.

How different it feels when your vow of devotion means, "I will not get involved with anyone else so long as our relationship continues. If we become so unhappy with one another that we cannot work out our problems, we may have to end our relationship. Only then, will I allow myself to take on another romance." This act of devotion is undertaken with full understanding that there will often be temptations to resist.

Don't make promises you can't keep.

IN SOME situations, an open show of anger may not change anything. But, it can be crucial that we let others know when we feel angry.

Expressing anger is justified when others hurt us needlessly. We would prefer they treat us well out of love and respect, but when they don't, it's better for us to express our annoyance openly than to disguise underlying feelings of hurt or helplessness. We have to try to survive intact even when we can't count on someone else's caring.

At such times, we may have to settle for protecting ourselves by giving them a clear message that we are upset. Even if expressing our anger doesn't stop them, it may help us to retain our self-respect.

Expressing our anger may not intimidate our opponents, but it's often good for our digestion.

December 16

PEOPLE ARE often engaged in situations that require they play by the rules. In business, sports, and even in personal relationships, we agree to play fair, fulfill our contracts, and act in good faith.

However, there are some forms of play that involve solitary musings, games of self against chance, or isolated bits of secret whimsy. Because they have no impact on others, we need not play by the rules.

Still other kinds of play require that at least one other person be involved, but even then, there may not be any predetermined rules to follow, and no need to remind each other not to be so serious because "it's only a game." The best examples are conversation and lovemaking.

Intimate involvement between two people is a process of discovering what the rules between them are to be.

SOME OF us find it difficult to trust other people. For one reason or another, we are suspicious of their motives. Ironically, we usually distrust them when they act as if they like us. Then we wonder what they're up to. We only trust that they are being honest when they disapprove of our actions or seem put off by our attitudes.

When we first meet someone, if something we feel inside suggests that this person can't be trusted to treat us well, we blame ourselves for being defensive. When we ignore our gut instinct and make excuses for the stranger, we set ourselves up for allowing mistreatment we might otherwise have avoided.

Trust and distrust work best when they address both good and bad experiences.

December 18

WHEN WE promise someone that our love will last forever, all we're actually doing is expressing how much he or she matters to us right now. By tomorrow, or even later today, we may feel anger just as intensely as the love we professed. Then, we wonder what is wrong with our relationship.

Very likely nothing is wrong, but what may be missing is the understanding that there are certain to be times when we hate the one we love. And the more our loved one means to us, the more effort it's worth investing to try to work out our conflicts. Even when our feelings evolve from rage to coldness to nothing, if we can be patient enough to wait until there's an easing of the impasse, we'll feel love again, maybe with a sense of added depth, realizing we suffered through a really difficult time and still want to be with each other.

Ask your mate whether or not he or she is happy that you are together. If the answer is, "Sometimes," the two of you are doing pretty well.

Even imperfect love can be sufficient to make people happy much of the time.

SOME OF us feel so powerless about our emotional impact on other people that often unwittingly we are far more heavy-handed than we intend to be. We expect that, unless we exaggerate, other people won't pay any attention to what we have to say.

Paradoxically, when we carry on in extravagant displays of temper or self-pity, it is our overkill that keeps people from taking us seriously. For example, if we feel that someone has been less considerate than we would have wished, we whine that they have broken our hearts, or we strike back at what we experience as a slap in the face by condemning them as completely cruel and uncaring.

When we become captive of our own overblown metaphors, we find it easy to justify our counter-attacks. In the midst of the desperation that we experience as our helplessness, we are likely to treat the person who has offended us much worse than they treated us.

Beware of mistaking metaphors for the experiences they were intended to express.

December 20

THE IDEAL of improving ourselves is a wonderful servant and a terrible master. We probably feel better when we are attempting to improve our lot, but we can get trapped on the treadmill of never taking time off to enjoy how far we've come.

In the long run, perhaps progress is an illusion, as each achievement presents the next obstacle we must overcome. For example, if we overcome financial irresponsibility by careful planning, so that we no longer have to worry about paying off the debts, by then we may have forgotten how to be impulsively indulgent.

Each solution creating its own problems is a process someone once termed "technological redundancy." An example was given of a time when people lived unsheltered in an arctic environment so extreme that they had to build a big box in which to live. After a time they found that the warmth provided by the house spoiled the food they kept in storage. To save the food, they built a small box within the larger one. But soon they found that in the cooler they'd built, the butter was too cold and too hard to spread. To warm the butter, they built an even smaller box. This they called a butter-keeper.

There is no final solution to life's problems.

MOST OF us spend a great deal of time working for a living. We start out working to live, but many of us end up living to work. For some, the success we seek gets determined by other people's standards. For others, a sense of being unsuccessful comes from some longing in our souls that work never seems to satisfy.

Some people are trapped by lack of opportunity. It's one thing to be broke and another to be poor. Some of us needlessly trap ourselves by maintaining an arbitrary boundary between working and the rest of our lives.

For those of us fortunate enough to have the luxury of making our own vocational choices, success is choosing to do what we most want to do, doing it the way we most want to do it, and getting paid for being who we want to be.

Success is what we think it is.

December 22

ON THOSE cheerless dawns when we begin the day feeling gloomy we may not have a clue as to what it is that troubles us. We may recognize that the problem is simply that we're depressed, but when we try to reassure ourselves that after a while we'll feel better, our depression answers, "So what!"

On some of those awful mornings, our pessimism may be the result of being too tired and it will pass once we get the rest we need. Other times, we're marginally ill, perhaps with the beginning of a cold. When we get well, everything will feel okay again.

More often, our bad mood is a signal that there is a personal problem we haven't yet faced. As awful as depression may feel, it slows down life enough to offer us an opportunity to attend to the unpleasant issues that we've foolishly chosen to avoid.

Depression is an opportunity for reflection.

WHEN IT comes to solving problems, we each have our own style. For example, when faced with a dilemma, some people work hard at figuring it out before making a decision. Others trust their gut reactions and plunge into action.

No single approach is appropriate for solving every kind of problem. Unless we have a flexible attitude, we will fail more often than we might otherwise.

At times, we need to abandon what seems natural, only because it has become automatic. If we don't want our ways to grow into chronic rigidities, sometimes we must be willing to go against our grain. If instead we stubbornly insist on always doing it our way, we may die trying.

If we don't confuse how we do things with who we are, we will feel freer to make such shifts. Being wrong can be a helpful, humbling experience. Acceptance of the times that our way of doing things doesn't work requires both acknowledging our own frailties and appreciating others' strengths.

Sometimes it helps to try out not *doing it our way.*

December 24

FOUR CENTURIES after Christ was born, certain holy men went on long spiritual pilgrimages. Only a few names have been remembered, but the impact of these Desert Fathers lives on.

These abbots chose to live in desert caves, committing their gaze to eternity, their habits to austerity, and their selves to solitude. Paradoxically, their ways taught us more about everyday life among others than about eternity. They taught people to evaluate their experiences more by quality than length of time. Focusing on the depth each moment can bring us means to become eternal, hour by hour, in this world.

When men came to the Desert Fathers for guidance, the reply would be simple, direct, and personal. A story tells of a brother who came to one Abba Poemen asking, "Do you wish me to command the other brothers I live with?" "Not at all," the abbot replied. "Act first, and if they wish, they will follow your example." "But they have asked me to command them," the brother said. "No," the old man answered, "become a model, not a lawgiver."

Offer others your example and leave it to them to learn what they need to know.

WE OFTEN speak of faith as a power *outside* ourselves, a power greater than ours alone. We claim to believe in this power without physical evidence and label events we cannot explain as miracles. There is another way of having faith and believing in miracles that neither requires nor excludes a personal God and the sacred writings that allow us to hear His words.

Faith opens us to the higher power that lies *within* each of us and the miracles that our experience of life provides. Pearl Buck describes it this way: "I have no need for any other faith than my faith in human beings. Like Confucius of old, I am so absorbed in the wonder of earth and the life upon it that I cannot think of heaven and the angels."

When we act in accord with both our heads and our hearts, everything we do becomes a form of prayer.

December 26

SOMETIMES WE must experience pain to the limits of what we can endure before we are able to question what is appearance and what is reality. It is so easy to be tempted to stay stuck in a limited life role that offers little reward beyond its safe sense of familiarity. Sometimes we don't even realize we can change. And often when we do, no matter how dangerous the consequences of staying in the role, we prefer it to the risk of trying something new. In an unfamiliar, who-knows-what-will happen-next improvisation, we might not be able to handle the unpredictable outcome.

Even when we feel able to cope, yet another block is our vision of ourselves in relation to others. Their expectations of us usually hinder, rather than help us, and so trying new freedoms often requires that we give up hope of an appreciative audience.

For some of us, at some times in our lives, it is not possible to free ourselves without having someone we can count on to stand by and help, someone who cares about us, but not about how we choose to live.

Everyone feels lost and alone at times.

GROWING OLDER presents some of our most perplexing questions. We have heard the advice to grow old gracefully, but what does that mean we are supposed to do? The business of advancing age always presents us with something new.

Aging is an inevitable tide that cannot be turned. The everyday erosion of our physical strength is only one of the insidious inroads into our power. In addition, we cannot control sickness battering our bodies.

Even so, we are able to remain in charge of how we live our lives. And when we recognize that we have no choice in the matter of getting older, we are freer to accept the downside more easily.

Only God knows what He had in mind when He graced us all with gradually growing old and eventually dying. Why He chose some of us to stay healthy and strong and others to endure decades of illness, we will never have any idea. What advice can we offer others? It's pointless to tell them, "Don't get sick!" or "Don't grow old!" Some things we know, but can't change. Some things we can't know until we have the experience.

Learning to grow old gracefully brings out the best in us.

December 28

EXCESSIVE HOPEFULNESS insists on a dream of perfection that robs us of the power to confront every adult's lifelong struggles with the imperfect situations we must face. Like overriding fears, exaggerated hopes draw us into needless disappointments.

Hope is not trust. Hope is insistence that things will turn out the way we wish without acknowledging that living this way results in one disappointment after another. It is not that overly hopeful people have learned to cope in ways that will predictably bring about positive results. It is simply that they want what they want and these now-grown, desperately hopeful children imagine that, in the end, everything will turn out just fine. Although you may find it helpful to hope, learning to cope is more likely to get you what you want out of life.

Hoping is waiting. Coping takes work.

SINCE WE must all be fools at times, why not learn to be wise fools?

In *In Praise of Folly*, Erasmus wrote about the paradox of the wise fool who continues to foster self-acceptance. His protagonist Folly satirically challenges the wisdom of the powerful princes and clergy of her time, while boasting of her own failings. Like Socrates, her only claim to wisdom is that she knows that she knows not.

By accepting the fool in yourself, you open your imagination to possibilities that you were once too wise to consider. If feeling foolish is the price of trying out unorthodox ideas, the discomfort usually seems worthwhile.

In becoming a wise fool, you're really shifting from external rules to inner guidelines, and in doing so, you redefine all principles in accordance with your own perspective. As Zen Buddhists point out, "A petty fool is nothing but a worldling, but a great fool is a Buddha."

None of us can afford to miss opportunities to take charge of ourselves and to laugh and enjoy what we can.

December 30

APART FROM the clutter created by both our honest errors and by our deliberate irresponsibility, we can each bring to our lives some small measure of effective management. But no matter how wisely and carefully we may try to conduct our lives, much will happen that is beyond our personal control. Each of our lives will be determined largely by disinterested forces, and each will be ended by the impersonal inevitability of death.

All of us suffer total responsibility for a life over which we have only partial control. While we each lack sufficient freedom to feel fully in charge of our lives, even so, everyone must find ways to make this ultimately unmanageable existence personally meaningful.

Much of life remains beyond control. Unable to cope successfully with fate's unpredictable excesses, we are left feeling helpless and hopeless. Sometimes there is nothing we can do to make the situation right, no matter how hard we try.

Life is not a matter to be managed.

WHERE DID the universe come from? How and why did it begin? What is our place in it and where did we come from? In *A Brief History of Time*, Stephen Hawking considers these questions and ends up concluding that if we ever find the answers, "It would be the ultimate triumph of human reason—for then we would know the mind of God."

Until we do know, we must live without knowing. But our plight is far from hopeless, for it is the tension from uncertainty that provides the impetus and the creativity for us to live our own lives. In the absence of restrictive directives, and without wondering what other people think of the way we work, we are free to be original.

A story tells that after the death of a religious leader, his son took his place. However, when members of the congregation complained that the young man's ways were different from his father's, the son replied, "I am doing just as my father did. He did not imitate and neither do I."

 Lacking final answers, we are free to continue our search.

Sit finis libri, non finis quaerendi.

Let this be the end of the book, but not
the end of the searching.

—THOMAS MERTON

Index

388

392

393